# The Teaching of the Epistle to the Hebrews

*by*

## Geerhardus Vos, Ph.D., D.D.

Late Professor of Biblical Theology
in Princeton Theological Seminary

Edited and Re-written by
JOHANNES G. VOS, TH.M., D.D.

The Presbyterian & Reformed Publishing Company
Nutley, New Jersey
1975

# THE TEACHING OF THE EPISTLE TO THE HEBREWS
by GEERHARDUS VOS

Edited and Re-written by
JOHANNES G. VOS

*Copyright, 1956, by*
*Wm. B. Eerdmans Publishing Company*

PRINTED IN THE UNITED STATES OF AMERICA

# The Teaching of
# The Epistle to the Hebrews

## PREFACE

This volume presents my father's classroom lectures on the Teaching of the Epistle to the Hebrews. These lectures were delivered repeatedly by the author to his students in Princeton Theological Seminary. From time to time they appeared in mimeographed form. Most recently they were issued in duplicated form by the Theological Seminary of the Reformed Episcopal Church, Philadelphia, Pa. For the present publication in book form the material has been edited throughout and at many points verbal changes have been made in the interest of readability or clarity. At no point has the thought-content intended by the author knowingly been changed.

Those who are interested in a longer and somewhat more technical study of certain aspects of the teaching of the Epistle to the Hebrews are referred to the following articles by my father which appeared in *The Princeton Theological Review*:

*The Priesthood of Christ in the Epistle to the Hebrews,* Vol. V (1907), pp. 423-447 and 579-604.

*Hebrews, the Epistle of the Diatheke,* Vol. XIII (1915), pp. 587-632; Vol. XIV (1916), pp. 1-61.

JOHANNES G. VOS

Beaver Falls, Pennsylvania
January 15, 1956.

# CONTENTS

# The Distinctive Character of the
# Epistle to the Hebrews

# CHAPTER I

## THE DISTINCTIVE CHARACTER OF THE
## EPISTLE TO THE HEBREWS

The reader of the Epistle to the Hebrews is immediately impressed with the prominence of Old Testament forms of religion in this Epistle. There are two possible ways in which this fact may be explained. It is possible that the original readers were people who actually appertained to the system of the Old Testament. Or, on the other hand, it is possible that Old Testament forms of religion are prominent in this Epistle because the original readers, though not Jews, could best be taught certain lessons of truth by means of forms of religion found in the Old Testament.

The first of these possible explanations involves the idea that the original readers were Jews. This view has been held in two forms: first, that they were Jewish Christians living in Palestine; and second, that they were Jewish Christians living in the Dispersion. On the first of these alternatives — that the original readers were Jewish Christians living in Palestine — there are three possible views of the matter, which are as follows: (1) The popular conception; (2) the view of Bleek; and (3) the conception of Riehm. With reference to the view that the original readers were Jewish Christians of the Dispersion, we shall see that this view is not *a priori* impossible, and we shall test the argument in favor of it and shall consider the arguments that have been advanced against it.

Taking up the matters outlined above in detail, we may say at the outset that the outstanding feature of the Epistle to the Hebrews is its connection with the Old Testament and the prominence of the Old Testament in it. In answer to the question *why* the Old Testament is so prominent in this Epistle, one answer commonly given is that it is very obvious that the people addressed in the Epistle were Old Testament people themselves, who therefore were thoroughly familiar with the Old Testament. It is said that without such practical acquaintance with the Old Testament the original readers could not have been expected to be interested in this Epistle.

Another and a more recent view of this matter, however, is that worked out by Von Soden, which has also been espoused by Zahn. It is a view, therefore, which is held not only by liberal scholars, but also by conservatives. This view is that the original readers of the Epistle were not Jews at all, but Gentiles.

We shall consider first the older and more popular view, namely that the original readers were Jews. This view exists in two forms, which are differentiated by a geographical distinction. According to one form of this conception, the original readers lived in Palestine; according to the other form, they were Jews living in the Dispersion. With respect to the view that they were Jews living in Palestine, this again is subdivided into two different conceptions: first, the popular conception, namely that these people lived in Palestine, but as Jews had ceased some of their former practices, not carefully observing the sacrificial law; thus they became more like plain Christians; but at the time of the writing of the Epistle, they were in danger of drifting back into Judaism. Therefore the writer of this Epistle holds up before them the Old Testament in order to show them what it really is and how it falls short of the New Testament standard.

Concerning this view, we may say that it seems to rest on a misapprehension of the actual state of affairs, and does not meet the practical tests that may be applied. The early Christians of Palestine did not make an immediate and clean-cut break with the practices of Judaism. We find evidence of this, for example, in the reputation of James the Just in Eusebius. These people, therefore, had never yet really abandoned the forms of the ceremonial law. The great break with these forms came only with the destruction of the temple. And to locate the date of the Epistle *after* the destruction of Jerusalem would make it too late to be plausible.

The second form of this view, which has a far better historical background, is that of Bleek. Bleek's view is that this reaction toward Jerusalem and Judaism on the part of the early Jewish Christians living in Palestine had a concrete occasion, which resulted in the people being frightened, as it were, back toward Judaism. They noticed themselves becoming liberalized. Especially they noted the increasing liberalization of Jewish Christians living in the Dispersion. Therefore those living in Jerusalem began to fear the effects of Christianity, and fell back to Judaism in order to avoid the consequences of liberalism. We may regard this view as partly true, for it is generally accepted that the Jews of the Dispersion were more liberal than those of Palestine. This does not mean, of course, that they were unorthodox. However, so far as the Epistle to the Hebrews itself is concerned, it contains no proof whatsoever of Bleek's view, nor any evidence for such a distinction between the two spheres of Jewish Christendom.

The third form of the view, and the most acceptable, is that of Riehm, who says that the fault of these Jewish Christians living in Palestine lay not so much in their observance or non-observance of the forms of the ceremonial law, as in their mental attitude. Riehm's conception is that they were offering sacrifices with an essentially self-righteous attitude of mind. Thus they lacked a proper appreciation of the sacrifice of Christ. This self-righteous state of mind Riehm attributes to a deeper fault, namely to their *religious externalism* — their desire for feeling and handling things. From such an attitude of externalism, Riehm feels, came their predilection for the Jewish rites. He traces this out not only in the Epistle's treatment of the sacrifices, but also in certain intimations that the readers had an over-expectation of the return of the Lord, a too great interest in eschatology. Thus they became unbalanced in both of these ways as a result of their religious externalism. To Riehm's diagnosis of symptoms and cause we may provisionally agree. But we do not follow Riehm in his theory as to *how* the original readers of the Epistle had contracted this "disease" of religious externalism. His explanation is that it was because they had been Jews living in Palestine. The objection to this last position, and consequently to the whole Palestinian view, is chiefly based on the geographical element, as we shall now endeavor to make clear.

First, in 2:3 we discover that the people addressed had been converted by those who had personally heard the Lord; therefore the original readers were *second generation* Christians. Could this be unequivocally affirmed of the Christians living before the year 70? Then in 6:10 the writer of the Epistle commends the readers for their liberality in ministering to the saints. But we know that the church at Jerusalem was itself an impoverished and needy church. Its members had to be ministered unto, and hence were not in a position of ability to minister to others. Note, too, the fact that those to whom the readers had ministered are called "saints." While "saints" was of course a term applicable to all Christians, still it was also a semi-technical term applied to the Christians at Jerusalem. They were the saints *par excellence*. For these reasons we cannot regard the original readers of the Epistle as Jerusalem Christians.

Still a third argument against Riehm's view may be derived from the language. The language in which the Epistle was written was not Hebrew or Aramaic, which would be expected in an epistle written to Jews living in Jerusalem. But the Epistle to the Hebrews is written in Greek. Moreover, its literary style refutes the argument that the Epistle as we now have it is a translation into Greek from an Aramaic original. Note, for example, the play on words in certain places in the Greek text, as in 5:8, *emathen aph' hoon epathen.* Also it is improbable that the writer of the Epistle was unable to write in Aramaic, had that been preferable for the sake of his readers, since he was so thoroughly acquainted with everything else Jewish.

But if the original readers were Jews of the Dispersion, then all the above arguments fall away. This theory must therefore be investigated on its own merits. There can be no *a priori* objection to it. There were many very strict Jews in the Dispersion. This strictness did not come to an end even with the destruction of the temple. The Epistle of Barnabas sheds light on this point; it is quite probable that they expected an early rebuilding of the temple.

We shall now proceed to consider the argument derived from the manner of addressing the people. They are called "the people of God." It is said that this must refer to Jewish Christians, on the basis of Old Testament usage and terminology. But this argument is not conclusive. For the expression may equally well have arisen out of the universalism of the writer. The apostle Paul, for example, in writing to Gentile Christians, used similar terms. And the writer of the Epistle to the Hebrews was probably very intimately connected with Paul. Thus Paul says to the Corinthians (1 Cor. 10:1), "All our fathers were under the cloud, and all passed through the sea"; and to the Romans (Rom. 4:16), "Abraham, who is the father of us all;" and to the Galatians (Gal. 4:26), "Jerusalem which is above is free, which is the mother of us all."

A further argument is drawn from 9:15, "And for this cause he is the mediator of a new covenant, that a death having taken place for the redemption of the transgressions that were under the first covenant, they that have been called may receive the promise of the eternal inheritance." It is alleged that the writer of the Epistle would not have called the readers' attention to this fact if they had not already had an interest in it. This sounds plausible, and we would have to adopt this view, except for the fact that we find another motive for the introduction of the subject in the context in chapter 9 of the Epistle. It is this: that the covenant is so superior as to have even a retroactive power, extending back to the first covenant. That this is the preferable exegesis appears from the fact that the writer in 9:15 does not use the second person but the third.

Again, in 6:1 and 9:14 we find the phrase "dead works." This expression has been understood by many as referring to the law works of the Old Covenant. One of the first principles had been repentance from these, and cleansing in Christ's blood. But this interpretation involves a serious difficulty, since the opposite of "dead works" is said to be "the living God," so that the contrast is to the false gods of paganism. Thus the contrast takes this form: *dead works* versus *worship of the true God.* Moreover, there is no indication in the Scriptures that the Old Testament works of legal obedience, as such, required repentance or cleansing; they were works commanded by God, only they were inadequate because they fell short of satisfaction. Therefore we conclude that the expression "dead works" means, not works of law observance, but sinful works — works defiling a person as contact with the dead defiles.

The passage 13:9-13 seems to have most to contribute to this view. We must distinguish here two points: (1) the solicitation of the readers: from what quarter does this solicitation come? (2) to what race or class is the solicitation addressed? The writer begins by saying, "Be not carried away by diverse and strange teachings." Now this cannot refer to the observance of the Jewish law. The teachings of the Old Testament could not be regarded by Gentile Christians — much less by Jewish Christians — as "diverse and strange teachings." The reference must be to something peculiar. Fortunately other parts of the New Testament afford some help in this difficulty, namely Romans 14, Colossians 2:1 and 1 Timothy 4. In these passages we note references to what might be called *ultra*-legalism: an attempt to do something over and above the requirements of the Jewish law. Evidently this is also the case in Hebrews 13; therefore the solicitation came from Jewish quarters. Still it did not come from a general Jewish source, but from a particular circle who went beyond the actual requirements of the law.

This solicitation could not have come *to* Jews as readers of the Epistle, for the writer says, "Be not carried away," implying that they had *not formerly* been occupied by these strange teachings. Still, this does not settle anything as to their race. We should remember, however, what is meant by the expression "diverse and strange teachings." The passage continues: "It is good that the heart be established by grace; not by meats (*broomata*)." If this is related to sacrificial meals, the argument in favor of Jewish readers will have to stand. But this word (*broomata*) is never so used. In the LXX it always refers to a law of clean or unclean foods; therefore we conclude that here also it must refer to a certain asceticism of abstinence. This again leaves undecided the question as to who the original readers were.

Coming now to 13:9 *ad fin.,* we read: "wherein they that occupied themselves were not profited." Note the use of the third person here, indicating that the readers themselves had never personally walked in these things. But this still does not determine the question as to who the readers were. Going on to 13:10, we note in the original text the emphasis on the verb, which stands first in the sentence: "We have an altar, whereof they have no right to eat that serve the tabernacle." Note the introduction of a new element here, carrying the fight into the lines of the enemy, as it were, as if to say, "They have no right to practice *your* religion; those people have no right to partake of the blessings of the Christian's service." Note that the author refers to the opponents as those "that serve the tabernacle"; they are therefore the Jews. But the form in which it is put also proves that *the readers were not Jews.*

Verse 11 is simply an elaboration of verse 10. The writer is here arguing typologically. The sacrifices had to be burnt without the camp; the Jews therefore had no right to *eat* of this highest sacrifice, a fact which had already been foreshadowed by the law. Finally, verse 12 proves the same

principle in a different form. Jesus made *His* sacrifice one
of that kind of which the Jews had no right to eat. The
argument here is both from the typology and from the actual
fulfillment.

Thus we see that the argument, while having something to
do with Jewish practices, is such as would be addressed to
Gentile Christians. Therefore we conclude that the arguments used in support of the opposite view are without force.
Moreover, one passage (6:1) even makes that view *impossible*.
The writer there speaks of the *first principles* in which the
readers had been instructed when they *first became* Christians. These first principles were: repentance, faith, baptism,
laying on of hands, resurrection and eternal judgment. Now
the Jews did not have to be instructed in these elementary
matters, since they knew them from the beginning. A convert
from paganism, however, would have to be taught the meaning of repentance, faith, etc. This is also borne out by
several subsidiary facts. For one thing, consider the terms
in which the writer speaks of the threatened apostasy. These
terms are too strong to be used in the case of a Jewish Christian falling back into Judaism; they indicate a fall to the very
bottom: 3:12, "falling away from the living God"; this would
not be true of a Jewish Christian lapsing back into Judaism.
Also note 3:13, "the deceitfulness of sin"; 10:26, "sinning
wilfully"; 10:29, "treading under foot the Son of God." This
last statement could, to be sure, also be made of a Jewish
Christian falling back into Judaism. Still, most of the statements quoted are applicable only to an apostasy into paganism.

Again, when the writer draws a comparison between the
Old Testament and the New Testament, he never turns it
to account to warn the readers *away* from the Old Testament.
He uses it only to show the *superiority* of the New Testament;
for example, in 2:2 the angels and Christ are contrasted.
The angels are the highest conceivable created beings, yet
Christ stood out as superior to them. The Old Testament
economy was superintended by angels. The writer does not

say that it is folly to fall back into that system, but he does urge the need of a greater heed now, because of the higher object.

In the third chapter, again, the writer compares Moses and Christ. If his purpose was to warn the readers against the service of Moses, we would have a contradiction here. For it was precisely those *who did not obey Moses* that fell in the wilderness. It might be said, of course, that the writer is here simply actuated by motives of good policy, not to depreciate the Old Testament but rather to hold up the New Testament as being something better. But if this were his real motive, we might have expected at least some slip on his part here and there in the Epistle.

Further, we note the detachment of the argument in the Epistle from the chronology of the time of writing. The representation in this Epistle deals with the Mosaic age, with the tabernacle, not with the temple which existed when the Epistle was written. It is true that the sacrifices are spoken of in the present tense, as then being observed, but this is proper to the form of argumentation, which presents that which the tabernacle ritual *is*. It is not the present tense of chronology, but of legal validity, that is being used. That *is* the law; according to the law this or that *is* what is prescribed. So we read in 10:1, 2, "For the law having a shadow of the good things to come, not the very image of the things, *can* never with the same sacrifices year by year, which they offer continually, make perfect them that *draw* nigh." Here we have three verbs all in the present tense, yet this does not imply that the sacrifices are now being offered year by year. Rather, the writer means that *according to the prescriptions of the law* the sacrifices can never cease, but must be repeatedly offered. This involves no reference to their actual observance in his day.

We need not concern ourselves with the question of the probable domicile of the original readers of the Epistle, since this question is of no importance if the readers were Gentile Christians, as we have now concluded that they were.

This view that the original readers were Gentile Christians is a more recent view than the others. It was first introduced by Roth in 1836. It was also held by Von Soden in 1884, and in more recent times it has been held by Moffatt and McGiffert. This view may borrow some parts of Riehm's argumentation, which held that the readers were Jewish Christians. While his conclusion is, in our view, incorrect, still his diagnosis is correct, namely that the condition of the original readers was one of *religious externalism*. This may be seen by a hasty survey. Note the opening verses of the Epistle. There is no introduction or salutation. This may be psychologically explained by the *urgency* of the case. The writer begins at once with, a piece of Christology touching upon two of Christ's offices, namely His priesthood and His kingship. Therefore we may conclude that the trouble with the original readers was in part, at least, Christological. What their particular Christological trouble was appears in the second chapter, namely, that Christ did not appear to them externally as they had expected. And they even found something objectionable in Christ's humiliation and sufferings. Therefore from 2:5 on, the reasonableness and necessity of Christ's humiliation is set forth. Note the terms used to express this: 2:10, "For it became him, for whom are all things, and through whom are all things, in bringing many sons unto glory, to make the author of their salvation perfect through sufferings." Thus Christ's humiliation is represented as something which should be *expected*. Also in 2:17 the same idea occurs: "Wherefore it behooved him in all things to be made like unto his brethren."

Thus we see that the original readers apparently did not appreciate the inner side of the importance of Christ. The author now shows that Christ's humiliation was necessary for His own sake, namely for His glorification. We see Him crowned with glory and honor, *because* of sufferings and death. Secondly, the author intimates that in not perceiving this honor and glory in Christ, the readers reveal their want or lack of this for themselves. Therefore he says in 2:10

that Christ's humiliation was necessary not only for *His* glory but also for *their* glory.

In chapter 3 we have the comparison between Moses and Christ. We should observe that this comparison issues in a long discourse (which, however, is not a *discursus*) on the subject of *the rest of God*. This is introduced to meet the readers' eschatological difficulties. The author warns them not to fall into the same type of unbelief as in the time of Moses. The source of this unbelief in Moses' day had been doubt as to the fulfilment of the promises of God. Now the original readers of this Epistle were suffering from an acute eschatologism. They were interested in eschatology even to the point of unbelief — unbelief because of the postponement of what they expected. The peculiar feature of eschatology is that it brings something *new*. It brings the eternal side of the promises of God. The author instructs the readers that they must rely less upon the fulfilment than upon the promise. What they need is an eschatology of faith, not an eschatology of imagination. The latter is the fault of all false eschatology, which seeks to picture the fulfilment of the promises in realistic detail. What the author calls upon the readers to do is rather to reduce the promises of God to their spiritual essence, as taught in the Word of God.

Thus we see that both in the matter of the humiliation of Christ and in the matter of eschatology, the hypothesis of religious externalism lying at the bottom of the readers' trouble seems to explain their condition.

The next topic in the Epistle is its treatment of the *priesthood* of Christ. The first reference to this is in 2 : 17, "Wherefore it behooved him in all things to be made like unto his brethren, that he might become a merciful and faithful high priest in things pertaining to God, to make reconciliation for the sins of the people." Here Christ's priesthood is connected with His humiliation, serving the purpose of making the latter palatable to the readers by showing that it was necessary. The relation of the priesthood to the readers' specific trouble may also be further seen in the emphasis laid on the fact of its being a *heavenly* priesthood.    It is exercised in heaven, in the Holy of Holies, out of the sight of the people.    This had been foreshadowed in the Old Testament by the entrance of the high priest into the Holy of Holies, out of the sight of the people.    So Christ also ascended out of their sight into heaven.    This also provoked criticism on the part of the readers, because the glory of Christ was not physically visible to them, being withdrawn from their sight.    The author of the Epistle shows that this, far from detracting from Christ's glory, really *adds* to it.    The author thus presents the opposite of what they were looking for as the really desirable thing.

Following the discussion of the priesthood of Christ, the Epistle takes up the topic of Christ's sacrifice.    The author holds up the *eternal, spontaneous, spiritual* character of the sacrifice of Christ.    In 9:14 Christ's sacrifice is compared with that of bulls and goats.    As the blood of the latter cleansed *externally,* so the blood of Christ cleanses *internally;* it cleanses the conscience.    But why or how is this so?    It is because Christ shed His blood spontaneously and spiritually. This fact again, therefore, was well fitted to counteract the religiously externalistic attitude of the readers.

Finally, we must see what the author says about *faith.* Paul usually represents the believer's faith as an external instrument, the instrument of justification, although not entirely so.    Thus he speaks of "walking by faith" as distinguished from "walking by sight."    Faith is the great spiritualizing principle, for faith is the state of mind that keeps us in touch with the higher world.    Therefore the author of the Epistle to the Hebrews speaks of faith as being "assurance of things hoped for, a conviction of things not seen" (11:1).    Thus there is a close connection between faith and hope.    There is such a thing as a hope of the imagination, which is merely externalistic.    But there is also a hope closely joined to faith, which goes straight to the root of things, to the promises of God.    This is the faith here spoken of.    The same point of view is also found in Peter, for example in

1 Peter 1:21, which we may correctly render thus: "that your faith might also be hope in God."

In connection with the subject of faith the writer also dwells at length on *patience under persecution*. This is connected with the same spiritualizing principle of faith. Patience is a term characteristic of the Stoic philosophy, but in Stoicism patience is sheer will power to hold out. We should note the etymological meaning of the Greek word for patience — *hupomonee* — meaning *to keep under,* that is, to keep the mind under and not be ruled by it. But Christian patience is not a suppressing of any powers; rather, it is a balancing of powers. There is another power which enters into the believer's life to offset the power of persecution. This new power comes to him through faith. And to this the believers of the Old Testament period had not yet attained.

# The Epistle's Conception
# of the Diatheke

# CHAPTER II

## THE EPISTLE'S CONCEPTION OF THE *DIATHEKE*

The Epistle to the Hebrews is the only New Testament epistle giving prominence to the term *Diatheke*. In Jesus' own discourses the word occurs only once (Matt. 26:28; Mark 14:24; Luke 22:20), in the formula "This cup is the new *Diatheke*." Paul uses it only in Gal. 3:4; 2 Cor. 3; Eph. 2; Rom. 9 and 11 — nine times in all. In Luke's writings, outside the above passages, it is found only three times: once in the Gospel (1:72), and twice in Acts (3:25 and 7:8). Only once more does it occur in the New Testament outside of the Epistle to the Hebrews, in Rev. 11:19. This makes a total of 16 occurrences in the New Testament outside of the Epistle to the Hebrews. And in Hebrews alone it occurs 17 times.

This naturally requires some explanation. Why should an idea so prominent in the Old Testament be so eclipsed in the New? A proximate explanation may be given, that other ideas take its place, namely the ideas of the Church and of the Kingdom of God. But the question still remains, *why* should this change have taken place? The answer is that through the coming of the Messiah the people of God have received a new form of organization taking the place of the *Berith* organization. This new organization yielded the ideas of the Church, Christ, and the Kingdom of God. The Covenant idea does not pass out altogether, of course, for it still requires an occasional reference in the New Testament.

But now the other question must be raised: why should the Epistle to the Hebrews be such a conspicuous exception, in this respect, to the general usage of the New Testament? In answer we may say that this depends first of all on the purpose of the writer. He proposes to compare the old order of things with the new. To do this, as in all cases where two things are to be compared, a common denominator is necessary. Now the *Berith* idea was the most suitable common denominator available. Hence the writer considers the new order also as a *Berith* or *Diatheke.* The only other possibility open to him would have been to use the idea of *law*, but this would not suit the genius of the New Testament writer. Only occasionally does this idea of law creep into the Epistle to the Hebrews, as for example in 7:12, "For the priesthood being changed, there is made of necessity a change also of the law"; and also in 8:6, "by so much more as he is also the mediator of a better covenant, which hath been *legally enacted* upon better promises."

Still, besides this special purpose of the writer, there is also the personal preference of the author at work in this matter. The peculiarity of the author's conception of religion is that it lies almost entirely in the sphere of consciousness. This may be contrasted with Paul's conception, which represents much of religion as lying *beneath* consciousness. Paul holds up the mystical aspect of union with Christ through the Holy Spirit, something which is wholly lacking in the Epistle to the Hebrews. The writer of Hebrews rather regarded only the *phenomenal* aspect of religion — a point important to remember in connection with the exegesis of the difficult and important passage 6:4-6.

The next question that presents itself is as to the *meaning* of *Diatheke.* In 9:16, 17 it is plainly given the meaning of *testament,* referring to the death of the person who has made it. This refers first of all, of course, to Christ. But then the author extends the idea also to the Old Testament, saying that even in the old *Diatheke* there was the symbol of death. From this it is easy, of course, to argue that the word *Diatheke* must mean *testament* everywhere. In defense of this position Riggenbach wrote a dissertation in 1908, in a volume of essays by different writers dedicated to Zahn. His thesis is entitled "The Conception of the *Diatheke* in the Epistle to the Hebrews." He holds to the uniform meaning of *Diatheke* as *testament*. The same idea is also worked out in his commentary on Hebrews in the Zahn series.

Because of the importance of this point, we shall digress to trace the idea through the whole of the Old Testament and the New Testament.

The trend toward translating *Diatheke* as *testament* is rather recent. In 1881, when the Revised Version was published, the tendency was still toward *covenant*. The word occurs 33 times in the New Testament. The Authorized Version renders it by *covenant* 21 times and by *testament* 12 times, thus showing a marked tendency toward the translation *covenant*. But the Revised Version allowed only two of the 12 cases to remain as *testament,* and translated by *covenant* in 31 cases. Still the possibility was reckoned with that *testament* might be the correct rendering, and therefore *testament* was placed in the margin, not only in the cases where the Authorized Version had *testament,* but also where the Authorized Version had *covenant*. The revisers therefore by no means settled the question. What moved them to favor the rendering *covenant* was no doubt their desire to maintain harmony between the Old Testament and the New Testament. For in the Old Testament there was no *testament* idea; therefore so far as possible the Revisers made the idea uniform throughout by translating the Greek word as *covenant*.

We may inquire, therefore, as to what it was that, during more recent years, has caused the commentators to veer around to *testament* as the correct translation of *Diatheke*. Doubtless this has been the result, not of comparison of the New Testament with the Old, but rather of purely linguistic considerations. The commentators asked what was the current meaning of the word in the Greek vernacular at the time of making the LXX translation of the Old Testament. It seems that at that time the word had the ordinary meaning of *testament*. This has been demonstrated by a study of the usage of the word in papyri and other sources. Now if the term *Diatheke* was already understood as *testament* in the LXX, then of course this meaning must have passed over also into the New Testament.

But what is the significance of this meaning of *testament* as over against *covenant?* The translators of the LXX of course wished to express by it the meaning of the Hebrew word *Berith;* it certainly was not their intention, in translating the Old Testament from Hebrew into Greek, to replace an old idea by a new one. On account of this some modern scholars have held that the translators of the LXX must have understood the word *Berith* in a wrong sense, for the Old Testament simply knows nothing of a *testament.* On this view the translators of the LXX must be regarded as having committed a double blunder: they not only concealed the true meaning, but also actually substituted a false meaning for it.

In itself this would not necessarily be serious to us, since the LXX is only a translation of the Old Testament and therefore is not held to be infallible as a version. But there is a connection between the LXX and the New Testament. For on the view of these scholars the New Testament itself is regarded as having inherited this blunder from the LXX. When the New Testament is thus accused of a blunder, the matter becomes a serious one to us, for we hold the Greek text of the New Testament to be infallible Scripture. To be sure, some of the modern advocates of this view are not troubled by this consideration, since they do not accept the infallibility of the New Testament. In some cases they are even happy over this alleged blunder, for they say that out of a linguistic evil a religious good has come to pass. They assert that in this matter the LXX translators rendered religion a signal service. *Berith,* they admit, meant *covenant;* but they regard the whole covenant idea as an ignoble conception, picturing the relation between God and man as a contract. On the other hand, in their opinion, the idea of *testament* substituted a very noble conception for the ignoble one: God disposes for Himself of His possessions according to His own good pleasure. Cf. Deissmann, who sets the LXX and the New Testament over against the Hebrew Old Testament as two distinct Bibles; also cf. Behm, who asserts that the idea of contract has in it the idea of synergism, which now gives way to the loftier idea of monergism. We must now consider what should be our attitude to these various ideas.

As far as the Old Testament is concerned in this whole judgment, a gross misunderstanding is involved. These scholars are so engrossed with linguistic studies that they fail to do justice to the facts. Accepting the rendering *testament* for a moment, must we hold that this is necessarily contrary to the Old Testament idea of *Berith?* It is far from true that *Berith* in the Old Testament uniformly means *covenant.* That view has long been abandoned by scholars. The idea of *agreement,* as a matter of fact, does not belong to the essential meaning of the word *Berith* at all. This does not mean, of course, that *Berith* cannot sometimes mean a covenant. The point is that it is not called *Berith* for that reason, but rather because it has a solemn religious sanction attached to it. It may in itself be either an agreement or a promise; the essential element of a *Berith* is the absolute confirmation of the arrangement, whatever this may be.

In numerous instances God alone makes the arrangement, and it is called a *Berith* because of the solemn religious sanction. For example, in Genesis 15, the first promise made to Abraham was *merely* a promise, but in the second stage God made a second promise, and upon the request of Abraham added a religious ceremony, by which He made the promise a *Berith.* Similarly, the promises made to Noah, accompanied by the sign of the rainbow, form a *Berith.* At Sinai, also, the agreement between God and Israel, being ratified by a solemn transaction, is a *Berith.*

A *Berith* may also be established by a conqueror over the conquered. The mere idea of *covenant,* therefore, by no means covers the essential meaning of the word *Berith.* To substitute a better term than *covenant* is, of course, a more difficult matter. Another instance of the peculiar meaning of the word is that the law has the idea of *Berith.* In Psalm

119 *law* and *Berith* are used interchangeably. The law could only be spoken of in this way by reason of the solemn religious ceremony which accompanied its establishment.

In conclusion, then, the idea of two-sidedness, as of a covenant, has no bearing at all on the essential meaning of the term *Berith*. As soon as we begin to appreciate the real meaning of *Berith* we see how high it is raised above the charges of some modern scholars.

Next, in classical Greek, it is said, the word *Diatheke* means only *testament*. But this assertion is too sweeping. The word is derived from *dia* and *titheemi*, which means to put something down at intervals, to make a *disposition* which discriminatingly allocates things, putting each in its proper place. Further, the middle voice means to do this for one's self, for one's own interest. The word *Diatheke*, therefore, etymologically and originally means *a disposition for one's self*. But this is a word which the lawyers worked on and robbed of its original meaning. They so impoverished it that it came to mean only disposition of one's property at death. The Greek mind, however, could never lose sight of the fuller meaning of the word. There are instances in Greek literature in which the richer meaning is preserved, as in Aristophanes, "unless they make a similar *arrangement* with me as that monkey made with his wife (*ei mee diathoontai Diatheke*)."

With regard to the LXX, the question is what the translators wanted the readers to understand, whether the narrow technical meaning, or the richer original meaning. They could hardly have applied to God the narrower meaning of last will and testament, since this involves the idea of death. In the special case of Christ, as we note in Hebrews 9, the word *is* associated with death, the death of Christ being well known. But this was not the case with the translators of the LXX. Moreover, if they had intended *Diatheke* to be understood as *testament,* there surely would have been some intimation, among the hundreds of instances of the usage of the word, to reveal the intended meaning. There were plenty of opportunities for this on their part. For example, the idea of

*Berith* and that of the inheritance of Canaan frequently go together. But the translators do not express it as if the inheritance were to be regarded as following *ipso facto* from the *Berith*. Besides, the construction which they use with this word must be noted. They use three different constructions, namely, *pros, ana meson,* and *meta*. Now, of these three, the last two do not fit the idea of *testament* at all, and the first fits it only very imperfectly. Also there are instances in which the translators of the LXX obviously understood *Berith* as synonymous with *law;* cf. Ex. 19:5; Deut. 29:9.

It is possible, of course, that the translators of the LXX, having to choose between *Diatheke* and *Suntheke,* chose *Diatheke* as the less of two evils. If they had used *Suntheke,* the misapprehension would have arisen that God and man are equal factors in the arrangement. But in the case of *Diatheke* there was the possibility of the word being misunderstood to mean last will and testament. The LXX translators had three possibilities open to them: (1) They might have used the word *Suntheke,* which means *agreement* or *covenant;* (2) they might use *Diatheke* with the prevailing meaning of *testament;* (3) they might use *Diatheke* with the original meaning of *disposition*.

Of course no word can ever be translated into another language exactly, with all the precision and nicety of meaning that it has in the original language. Translation must always remain a choice between relatively suitable words, a matter of selecting the best word from among those that are available. In the three possibilities before the LXX translators, as enumerated above, the disadvantages in each case were as follows: (1) Whereas *Suntheke* meant *covenant,* the original *Berith* did not always mean *covenant,* and even considering the cases where *Berith* did mean *covenant, Suntheke* would be unsatisfactory because the preposition *sun* with which this word is compounded gives the idea of synergism, which the original term *Berith* did not have. (2) In *Diatheke,* meaning *testament,* the evil involved is the association with the idea of death. Over against this evil, however, as compared with *Suntheke,* there is the advantage that a testament is one-sided, and therefore implies monergism. (3) Taking *Diatheke* in its older meaning of *disposition,* there was the disadvantage of the obsoleteness of the word. *Diatheke* with the meaning of *disposition* had the advantage, however, of not involving either of the two evils involved in the first two possibilities. Therefore, we may conclude, it was this third possibility that the LXX translators chose.

Next we shall proceed to the examination of the New Testament passages outside the Epistle to the Hebrews. The one passage that seems to contain the idea of *testament* exclusively is Gal. 3:15-17. Here Paul introduces the word *Diatheke* to express the idea of immutability. A *Diatheke,* he says, is unchangeable. And he uses this argument to prove the impossibility of the *Diatheke* being changed later by the law. This creates the presumption that Paul meant *testament* here. But even of *testament* we do not have the feeling of its necessary unchangeableness, since in our day a testament may be repeatedly changed prior to the testator's death. To remove this difficulty some have suggested that Paul's meaning was that none *except the testator* can change a testament. This cannot be Paul's argument, however, for his point is that not even God, the author of the testament, could change it at a later time. Thus it appears that Paul must have had a different kind of testament in mind from that with which we are familiar at the present day.

There was a type of testament which was absolutely unchangeable, even by the testator himself, namely the Syrian. This has been discussed by Ramsay in the *Expositor* for 1899. Paul could have had this type of testament in mind, which expressed precisely the idea which he required. That Paul actually did have this in mind follows from several considerations: (1) It is evident from the legal terminology which he uses, and which he could have avoided in many cases had he wished to do so, such as *kuroo, to confirm; akuroo, to render void; atheteo, to nullify; prokuroo, to confirm beforehand; epidiatassomai, to add something to what has been ordained.* (2) The prevalence of the idea of inheritance: Gal. 3:18; 4:1, 2, 3. Here, therefore, it is apparent that *Diatheke* must mean *testament;* therefore the Revisers erred in changing the rendering to *covenant* in this passage.

It might be said that Paul does not correctly render *Berith* as used in Gen. 15. In answer to this we must remember that an exact translation from one language to another is never possible. By rendering *testament* here Paul brings out beautifully the idea which was required, namely the *purpose* of the *Berith*, which was absolutely immutable.

The other passages where the rendering *testament* is possible are the narratives of the institution of the Lord's Supper in Matt. 26, Mark 14, Luke 22 and 1 Cor. 11. Many commentators, including Zahn, Deissmann and Dibelius, would also render *testament* in these passages, reading as in the Authorized Version instead of as in the Revised Version. They base their contention on the fact that Christ here evidently connected the covenant with His death. Through His death He thus *bequeaths* this covenant to His people. It is quite certain, indeed, that there is a close connection between the new *Diatheke* and Christ's death. But the testamentary idea is not the only way by which this connection can be introduced. For covenants and dispositions are often sealed with blood, as an inaugural sacrifice. The fact of the blood does not therefore decide the question.

Another argument is drawn from Luke 22:29, from the words spoken immediately after the institution of the Lord's Supper: "I *diatithemai* unto you, even as my Father *dietheto* unto me." If we give this verb the rendering of *bequeath*, and if we remember that the words were spoken immediately after the declaration "This cup is the new *Diatheke* in my blood," then it would seem to indicate that here *Diatheke* must mean *testament.* Still further, not only is the close proximity of the statement an argument for this, but also the fact that Christ here again speaks of eating and drinking, and that He speaks of their eating and drinking at His table in His kingdom. Thus also the thought of the preceding is apparently carried on; and, still further, there is the eschatological outlook.

To this argument, however, it may be answered that while Christ may properly be said to bequeath something to us, still it cannot be said of the Father that He dies and bequeaths something to Christ the Son. Therefore as we cannot hold to the rendering *bequeath* in the one case, we should abandon it entirely, and rather translate *appoint* as in the Revised Version. Also, the object of the verb does not meet the necessary requirements. We might possibly render this statement in two ways, either making *kingdom* the object of the verb, as that which Christ appoints for us, or making *eating and drinking* the object. If we adopt the former, we might keep the rendering *bequeath* and also retain the testament idea. But the sense is better if we take *eating and drinking* as the object, retaining *kingdom* as the object of the first verb only, being that which was appointed by the Father to the Son. *Eating and drinking* are not a suitable object of *bequeathing*, as the contents of a testament. As the second rendering is far the better, the whole imagery of testamentary disposition disappears from this passage.

In 2 Cor. 3 there is really nothing favoring the rendering *testament*. In this passage Paul contrasts his own ministry with that of Moses. It has been suggested that there is at least a hint of a testament here in the fact that Paul speaks of the *reading* of the old *Diatheke*. It has been attempted to explain this in keeping with the period of its writing, in that there were many of the apocalyptic writings which were spoken of as testaments, such as *The Testament of the Twelve Patriarchs*. Some have thought that Paul assimilates the Old Testament writings with these. This is not necessary, however. He could easily speak of the reading of the *Diatheke* as meaning the *Berith,* considering the fact that the latter is often synonymous with the *law*. That this is indeed the meaning is clear from what follows, where Paul speaks of Moses as being read, and implies therefore that

Moses is the author of it.  What Paul is contrasting here, then, is not two agreements, but two systems of endowment.

Gal. 4:24 closely resembles 2 Cor. 3, in that a contrast is introduced.  Here Paul uses an allegory, contrasting the two mothers, Hagar and Sarah, and the two localities, Jerusalem that is here on earth and Jerusalem that is above.  The one worship leads to bondage, the other to freedom.  Again, the one worship represents particularism and the other universalism.  Still there is a difference here from 2 Cor. 3. There Paul pictures the Old Testament and the New Testament as normally instituted by God.  But here Paul puts the New Testament and Christianity over against, not the Old Testament rightly understood, but the Judaism of his day which was a perversion of the Old Testament.  This may be seen from the fact that Hagar is represented as their mother. As to the meaning of *Diatheke* here, it is not *covenant* or *testament* but *disposition*.

In Rom. 9:4 and Eph. 2:12 the idea of *covenant* is plainly *excluded,* and likewise that of *testament* as we shall see.  In both of these passages the word *Diatheke* has the epexegetical genitive: *the Diatheke of the promise.*  The *Diatheke* itself therefore virtually is a promise.  This has been taken by some as a testament, because of the plural form.  This argument is without force, however, as the usage of the word elsewhere in the plural shows.  The plural here is meant by Paul as a real plural, meaning *promises.*  Paul is referring to the several promulgations of the divine promise in the Old Testament.

The only other Pauline passage concerned is Rom. 11:27, "And this is my covenant unto them, when I shall take away their sins."  This passage is complicated because it strings together three different passages of the Old Testament into a single quotation (Isa. 59:21; 27:9; Jer. 31:34).  Isa. 59:21 is distinctly a promise, as an assurance of the Lord to continue to give His Spirit, which Paul defines as being in substance the taking away of sins.

Besides the Pauline passages we still have one passage in the Gospel of Luke, two in the Acts and one in the Book of Revelation. In Luke 1:72 we read, "to remember his holy covenant." Here it is clearly the promise given to the fathers that is meant. In this case the statement preceding, "to show mercy toward our fathers," is almost a definition of the term *Diatheke* as here used.

In Acts 3:25, "Ye are the sons of the prophets, and of the covenant which God made with your fathers," we have virtually the same idea. Peter addresses the Jews by two names, as sons of the prophets and as sons of the covenant (*Diatheke*). The one, therefore, must serve to explain the other. *Sons of the prophets* here must mean *heirs* to what the prophets have given. So in the second case also, the idea must be *heirs of the Diatheke*. There is no reason, therefore, to think of *testament* here. The idea of inheritance here given is also too broad to demand the rendering *inheritance*. It has here a looser meaning of simply *obtaining*. It is curious to note that in the Old Testament passages referred to the *Berith* is not mentioned at all. Yet the two ideas lie so close together that Peter can call this promise, to which he refers, also a *Diatheke* in the same statement.

In Acts 7:3, "And he gave him the covenant of circumcision," Stephen speaks of the covenant of circumcision, referring to Gen. 17. This may be misleading, for we might be inclined to identify the *Diatheke* of which Stephen speaks with the *Berith* mentioned in Gen. 17. Stephen's meaning, however, is simply the law of circumcision. For we should note in Gen. 17 that the *Berith* is wholly on God's side, and the circumcision on Abraham's side, so that the command of circumcision is not a *Berith* in the sense in which *Berith* is used in Gen. 17. Therefore Stephen's use of the word *Diatheke* in connection with circumcision must be equivalent to *law*.

In Rev. 11:19, "there was seen in his temple the ark of his covenant," we have a very instructive example of the use of *Diatheke* as meaning *law*. Any other rendering would lead us far astray. This is similar to the usage in Heb. 9:4, "the tables of the *Diatheke*."

Returning now to the Epistle to the Hebrews, and beginning again where we broke off, at 9:16,17, it will be observed that here the word must mean *testament,* because of the reference to the death of the testator. The *Diatheke* does not avail so long as the testator liveth. An additional reason for this rendering, although it is not sufficient in itself, is found in the idea of inheritance. Third, we have here also the legal terminology: *pheroo, to bring something to the proper notice; bebaios, of force; ischuoo, to have validity; diathemenos, testator.* We think it impossible that any competent exegete should translate *Diatheke* in this context otherwise than as *testament.* Yet no less a scholar than Westcott does so. His view is as follows: while he cannot deny the fact of death in this passage, still he denies that the legal death of the testator is involved. He takes it rather as the idea of the death of a sacrificial victim, which is necessary as a ceremony for the establishment of a covenant. So far we might be able to agree with him; but the fatal objection to his view is that the death must be that of the person who made the *Diatheke.* To this Westcott answers that in every sacrifice in the Old Testament there is the idea of *representation.* The man who brings the sacrifice sees himself in the animal victim of the sacrifice. This is a plausible answer; but Westcott must also state the reasons for this strange reference here to the death of the man himself. To this he answers, that the writer was desirous of emphasizing *one* idea, namely the irrevocableness of the *Diatheke,* and this could not be expressed by simply speaking of the death of the sacrifice, hence the author speaks of the death of the man himself.

In criticism of Westcott's view, we may say that the whole idea of irrevocableness has been introduced into the passage by Westcott, an idea which he borrowed from the passage in Galatians. The idea uppermost in the mind of the writer in Hebrews 9, however, is not that the death makes the thing unchangeable, but that it makes it *effectual.* And secondly, if we were to apply this to Christ we would see that the idea is incongruous. Christ is the testator. But is it the teaching of the Epistle that Christ is now inoperative? No; just the opposite; His activity was not affected by death. It was precisely through dying that Christ acted, that He became a priest forever. We may, then, find these two ideas in the passage: (1) the death of Christ; and (2) through the death the thing became *ipso facto* operative.

This does not mean, of course, that the writer meant *Diatheke* as being in *every* sense an *only testament*. Rather, he uses this idea just for a moment, for a special purpose in this particular place. This may be seen in the verses immediately preceding and following. He is here moving not in the sphere of a testament, but in the sphere of a sacrifice. In verse 15 there is mention of redemption of transgressions, and in verse 18 likewise there is mention of dedication with blood, both of which are sacrificial ideas and not associated with *testament*. Verses 16 and 17 form a sort of parenthetical expression, therefore, which the writer employed for the sake of illustration, making momentary use of the double meaning of the word in current usage.

Discarding the rendering *testament* in the rest of the Epistle, we must decide which of the other two renderings — *covenant* or *disposition* — we shall employ. Both of these ideas seem to be connected with the word. For note the evident inclination of the author to emphasize the sovereignty and majesty of God, and His entire exclusiveness in setting things in motion: 3:4, "He that built all things is God"; 2:10, "Him, for whom are all things, and through whom are all things;" 13:20, 21, "Now, the God of peace, who brought again from the dead the great shepherd of the sheep . . . make you perfect in every good thing to do his will, working in us that which is well-pleasing in his sight. . ."

But which of the two renderings is the more in keeping with the intent of the writer? From the last quoted passage *Diatheke* would seem to mean a sovereign *disposal* of God. Another reason for this rendering is that where the making of the *Diatheke* is spoken of, the writer speaks of an *enacting*, representing God as the enacting Person: 8:6, "a better covenant, which hath been legislatively enacted (*nenomothetetai, laid down as law*) upon better promises." In 8:8 the writer uses *sunteleoo;* in 8:9, *poieoo;* in 9:20, *entelloo*. In this last passage it is striking to note that while the author is quoting from Ex. 24:8, he changes the Greek word from *diatithemi* which the LXX uses in that verse. He must have had some reason for this change; presumably the reason was his desire to bring out strongly the idea of a sovereign disposition.

Still further, the *Diatheke* appears as an institution with a view to a further end, not as an end in itself. This, of course, does not exclude the idea of *covenant*. Still, as it is concretely put, the end is stated, in which case the idea of *covenant* is not satisfactory. The end is usually stated as *teleioosis*. The *Diatheke* is a means to bring on perfection, not moral perfection, but the perfection of consummation, of bringing a person to his goal, to the ideal state. *Diatheke*, therefore, must be an institution or arrangement or disposition of God. That the *teleioosis* mentioned does not mean moral perfection is evident from the fact that it is used of Christ, of whom it cannot be said that He ever was morally imperfect; therefore in the case of believers also *teleioosis* must be understood in the sense of attaining to the end.

There are some passages which represent the *Diatheke* not as a means but as an end in itself. In these the connotation given is that of communion with God. In these cases the natural rendering would seem to be *covenant*. In 8:10 (quoted from Jer. 31:31) the writer speaks of a *Diatheke* between God and His people, in which He shall be to them a God and they shall be to Him a people. The nature of the *Diatheke* here is clearly that of a covenant.

Further, the nature of the relation of the people to God is that of a *latreia* (worship). According to 9:14, 15 this is the essence of the service of God.

In 13:20 we read of an eternal *Diatheke*. The description of it as eternal implies that it embodies the ultimate religious ideal. Here it is no longer a means, but an end in itself. Here, therefore, again, it is not merely a disposition, but a covenant.

Two conceptions naturally suggesting themselves as helps in determining the meaning of the word *Diatheke* are *egguos* and *mesites*. *Egguos* means *one who guarantees; mesites* means *mediator*. Now Christ is said to be the *egguos* and the *mesites* of the *Diatheke*. These words may at first seem to promise much help in determining the meaning of *Diatheke*, but, after all, the help they afford is rather meager. In classical Greek the word *egguos* does not enter into the legal terminology in connection with *Diatheke* at all. We may conclude, then, that the author is using the word in a non-technical sense. It means simply that Jesus guarantees the effectuation of the new order of things. With the word *mesites* the matter looks more promising. In our day the tendency would be to think of a *mesites* as a third person standing between the two parties of a covenant or agreement. But the word in the original has four different meanings, as follows: (1) The middle person between two contending parties; for this meaning see 1 Tim. 2:5. (2) A person with whom the contending parties deposit the object in litigation. (3) A witness in a lawsuit; from the verb *mesiteuo*, meaning *to bear witness in a lawsuit*. (4) A man who not merely guarantees the truth of a thing, but who guarantees the accomplishment of a promise or agreement.

It is plain that for us the choice must lie between the first and third meanings. The other two possibilities need not be considered here. But as between the first and the third, the most is to be said for the third. The chief reason for this is in 6:17, "Wherein God . . . *emesiteusen* with an oath." Here the author connected the word with God. God, therefore, acted as witness to the truth. The Revised Version renders here *interposed*. The Authorized Version is better, however, in rendering *confirmed*. Now if this is said of God, it is natural to attach the same meaning to it when it is asserted of Christ. We see, then, that the Epistle tends to treat the two words *egguos* and *mesites* as synonyms.

Finally, we must determine how the Epistle's idea of the *Diatheke* affects the whole of Christianity. There are two directions in which this may be traced: (1) the mode of the exercise of this religion; (2) the subject of this religion.

As to the mode, the Epistle considers the Christian state as in the main a *cultus*. Christianity is not a *douleia,* but a *latreia,* that is, a direct worship of God. This is intended in the sense of drawing near to God and worshipping Him. Note 12:28, where the Christian offers "service well-pleasing to God with reverence and awe"; 9:14, "to serve the living God." All through the ninth chapter the worshipper is represented as one who serves. This service is organized on the same principle as the Old Testament service. It is a service in a sanctuary, with priest, altar and sacrifice. The idea of sacrifice is wider, therefore, than that of atonement. Its essence is proper worship of God in His presence. The term used for this is *proserchesthai, to draw near*, as specifically conceived. We have here specifically ritual language. Note, for example, 4:16; 7:25; 10:1,22. This language is used not only of the believers, but also of the officers in the sanctuary, that is, of the priests. Back of this stands the idea that the priest *brings near* his sacrifice, as well as *bringing near* those who follow him. So we are brought near by Jesus as our High Priest and Forerunner. Then the believer also in his own life offers up himself, as we see in 13:13. Hence this Christian community has an altar for its sacrifice (13:10), at which altar Christ our High Priest ministers.

In another direction the work of Christ is designated by terms derived from this idea. It should be noted that these are distinctive from the Pauline terms. The Pauline terms of expression are such as *atonement, reconciliation, justification,* etc. But in Hebrews we find such terms as *purifies, sanctifies, renders perfect*. These terms are chosen because of the idea of approaching God and being rendered fit for service to Him. To that end we are relieved of disabilities, so that we may arrive at the goal of perfect worship. The point of view is, therefore, quite different from that of Paul. Paul describes the *process* of the atonement, whereas the author of Hebrews describes the *purpose* of the atonement. Of course these two viewpoints should not be regarded as contradictory in any way; rather, they are mutually complementary.

Christ is called for this purpose the *Sanctifier,* and believers are called *those who are sanctified*: 2:11; 10:19 ff. The latter passage emphasizes the importance of regular assembling of believers for the purpose of worship, because forsaking such assembling together means to deprive God of the worship which is His due.

Even the eschatological state of the people of God is viewed in the Epistle as a *cult* organization. The believers have come to Mount Zion and the city of the living God. . . and the spirits of just men *made perfect* — that is, just men who by their death have been made fit for this service (12:25).

The second point of this influence relates to the subject of religion. This is collectively conceived of in Hebrews, more than in any other New Testament document. As such a collective service is demanded, we cannot serve God individually. The Old Testament had already emphasized this truth; it made a *Diatheke,* and then engages *the people* to see to it that God receives His worship, at His stated time. This idea is here transferred to the New Testament. The author uses the same terms: 11:25, "people of God"; 2:17, "to make propitiation for the sins of the people"; 4:9, "there remaineth therefore a sabbath-keeping for the people of God"; 13:12, "Wherefore Jesus also, that he might sanctify the people through his own blood, suffered without the gate." The term *people of God* has no racial reference; those to whom it pertains are such on the basis of the *Diatheke.*

It remains to be stated that the author dwells on the social aspect of the *Diatheke.* This serves as a correction of false individualism, showing that we cannot serve God aright individually. The author describes the believers as the household of God, and this household is declared to be *one,* in both the old and the new *Diatheke,* 3:2-6. This has also an eschatological outlook, in the conception of *the city to come.* Note the description of the great eschatological assembly in 12:22. Thus it is affirmed of believers that they have not only joined in worship, but that they have been *incorporated* into the worshipping community.

# The Epistle's Philosophy of
# Revelation and Redemption

# CHAPTER III

## THE EPISTLE'S PHILOSOPHY OF REVELATION AND REDEMPTION

### 1. The Distinction between the Old *Diatheke* and the New

The Epistle distinguishes two *Diathekai*, the first being the Sinaiitic and the second that instituted by Christ. The first is referred to as the *Diatheke* made with the fathers, 8:9; note also 9:1-22. The second is called *a new Diatheke*, 8:8; *a better Diatheke,* 8:6; *an eternal Diatheke,* 13:20. The term *old covenant* is not found in Hebrews. As to the new covenant, it should be noted that the English adjective *new* is the rendering of two different Greek words, namely *kaine* and *nea.* The difference between these two terms is that *kaine* is retrospective, looking back upon the old; we in our day can still call the new covenant *kaine.* But *nea* means *recent,* or *still new;* and we of the present day can no longer regard the new covenant as *nea.* An instance of *nea* in connection with *Diatheke* occurs in 12:24.

We shall now consider the relation of the Abrahamic promises to both the old and the new *Diatheke.* With regard to the chronological delimitation of these two covenants, the old begins with Moses, not before, and ends with Christ. The author of Hebrews does not apply the term *Diatheke* to that which was transacted between God and Abraham. This distinction was not accidental, but was due to the fact that the author wished to establish the new *Diatheke* upon a double basis, namely upon the promise to Moses and the promise to Abraham; note 6:13, 14, 18.

The dividing point between the old *Diatheke* and the new is the death of Christ. The end of the old covenant and the beginning of the new covenant lies in the death, or perhaps

49

it would be more correct to say in the ascension, of Christ (7:11). The priesthood being changed, there is made of necessity also a change of *law.* The change of priesthood took place at the ascension, therefore it was then, also, that the change of the law took place, marking the initiation of the new covenant. According to 8:17 the new covenant has arrived when there is forgiveness of sins, and this is at the death of Christ.

In 9:10 we see that the time of setting things straight is when *the reality* comes, and the old is changed for the new. 9:15 is still more definite; the first covenant must be completely absolved, and redemption must take place through a death, before the new covenant can come. We may compare with this our Lord's words, "This cup is the new *Diatheke* in my blood," etc., showing that the new *Diatheke* comes at the point of His death. The author of the Epistle to the Hebrews simply stresses the priesthood somewhat more than the conception of sacrifice.

We shall now consider the identification of the two *Diathekai* with the two worlds eschatologically distinguished. The Epistle distinguishes not only two covenants, but also two worlds or ages, namely *this age,* and *the age to come.* The peculiarity of the old *Diatheke* is that it pertains to this present world, whereas the new *Diatheke* is that of the future eschatological world. The two terms, *Diatheke* and *world* are not exactly co-extensive, inasmuch as the world existed before the time of Moses. But the new *Diatheke* and the new world are co-extensive.

The writer in several instances affirms that believers are in actual contact with the world to come and its blessings. They are eschatological creatures. In 6:5 he states that they have tasted the powers *of the age to come.* In 9:11 and 10:1 he speaks of good things *to come;* and these good things to come are regarded as realized by the death of Christ. The writer affirms this not only in terms of time, but also in terms of place. The believers are situated where the eschatological world has its center. In 2:5 he speaks of *an inhabited world to come,* using a geographical term, *oikoumene mellouse.* The context shows what this *oikoumene* consists of: it is identical with the Christian's salvation. In 2:1-5 he exhorts them lest they neglect so great salvation; for "not unto angels did he subject the world to come." The salvation is so great, because everything is to be put under their feet. The world subjected to angels is the *old* world; the new is under the man Christ, and with Him is under all mankind.

This same idea is expressed in still another way in 12:22, where the author states that Christians have come to Mount Zion, the city of the living God, the heavenly Jerusalem. We miss the writer's meaning of this if we, regard this as a mere metaphor. Christians are really in vital connection with the heavenly world. It projects into their lives as a headland projects out into the ocean. This is a somewhat peculiar representation, but it is not confined to the Epistle to the Hebrews, for it is also found in Paul's writings. For example, in Phil. 3:20 Paul states "We have our commonwealth in heaven." Christians therefore are colonists, living in the dispersion in this present world. The same idea is set forth still more strongly in Eph. 2:6, "made us sit with him in the heavenly places," and also in Gal. 1:4, "that he might deliver us out of this present evil world." The Christian therefore is a peculiar chronological phenomenon. In Rom. 12:2 the apostle Paul draws the practical inference from this fact: Christians should be fashioned according to the world to come.

To Paul, the death and resurrection of Christ are the beginning of the world to come, and of the eschatological process. This conclusion followed necessarily from his teaching on the resurrection and the judgment, both of which began with Christ's death and resurrection.

The writer of the Epistle to the Hebrews has a special motive in his representation, however, being less doctrinal than Paul, and more practical. He sought to cure the readers of their religious externalism, and this externalism was attached to their distorted eschatology. They were dissatisfied because they did not as yet possess the external things, and therefore they were intensely interested in eschatology. The writer shows them that the eschatology is *present* for the most part, only certain features of it being reserved for the future. The internal, spiritual part is the important part, and this we have *now*.

There is a difference between Hebrews and Paul's Epistles not only in the motivation but also in the entire distinction. The representation of the present age is not the same in both. For Paul the present age is the *evil* age and the new age is the *perfect* age. Paul thus presents a bisection of universal history, with the resurrection of Christ as the dividing point. In Hebrews, however, the old age is the Old Testament. Thus Hebrews presents not a bisection of universal history, but a bisection of the history of redemption, which results, therefore, in a philosophy of redemption and revelation. The writer of Hebrews does not regard the old *Diatheke* as something evil, but rather as *the world of shadows* (the Levitical world).

Let us now glance at the Pauline passages, in order to note the ethical contrast presented in Paul's writings: Rom. 12:2; Gal. 1:4; I Cor. 1:2; 2:6; 2 Cor. 4:4 (the strongest statement of all, for it calls Satan *the god of this world*); Eph. 2:2, "the age (course) of this world"; Col. 1:13; 2 Tim. 4:10, "loved the present world."

In Hebrews there is reflection not on the ethical contrast between this world and the world to come, but on the inadequate, preparatory character of the one as over against the perfect, final character of the other. Another side of this matter is the fact that Hebrews does not drop the old usage altogether. The new remains in part still future: 13:14, "we seek after the city which is to come." The author speaks constantly of hope, as of something still in the future. Paul presents salvation in all three stages, past, present and future.

With respect to the ideas of *patience* and *faith,* we must now consider how these are to be reconciled. This is quite clearly presented in the Epistle. In principle, but in principle only, the coming age has already arrived. This conception is similar to that presented by Christ in His statements that the kingdom has come, and still must come. This may be called a semi-eschatological state of mind. The chronological aspect of the new age is only expressive of intense conviction of its reality on the part of the early Christians. We of the present day, having lost the realism, have also lost the sense of the soonness of its culmination. To be indifferent in regard to the time of this culmination is to commit a chronological sin. The normal Christian state of mind is to pray: "Come, Lord Jesus, come quickly."

Another solution offered for this problem of the twofold age is that the statements are to be regarded as Christological. Still others assert that the eschatological age has already come for believers, but not for unbelievers. The answer to this point of view, however, is that the whole is for believers only.

There are two passages in the Epistle in which it is not clear to which representation they belong. These are 1:2 and 9:26. The question is whether the new or future age, in these two passages, is regarded as beginning with Christ's ascension or with His return. In 1:2 we read that God hath spoken "in the latter part of these days" (*ep' eschatou toon hemeroon toutoon*) — not "in these last days" as in the Authorized Version. The expression *these days* extends back to the Old Testament and is distinguished from those days, which lie in the future. The concluding section of *these days* is now marked by the speech of Christ. The question is, how far do *these days* extend?

One interpretation is that they extend to the ascension of Christ. This is held to be the dividing point, so that everything after Christ's ascension, including the present life of believers, belongs to *those days,* that is, to the eschatological period. Another interpretation is that the speaking of the Son is not limited to the earthly ministry of Christ, but includes the whole Gospel preaching of apostles and ministers, so that it does not reach a conclusion until the end of time. Of these two interpretations the first seems rather preferable to the second, for the latter seems to make the "end of these days" too extended a period.

In 9:26 we read that Christ has been manifested *at the end of the ages*. This end was not just a moment, but a period of at least some duration. Again we face the question, how far does this end extend? The first interpretation is, again, that it extends through the ascension of Christ. In that case the writer and the readers of the Epistle were already *beyond the end of the ages*. But it is also possible to say that the manifestation of Christ is still going on. In that case we must regard the end of the ages as very protracted, extending even to Christ's second advent.

The distinction made between the present and the future age is of great importance in the teaching of the Epistle. The terms employed in this epistle are derived from the Mosaic institutions. Christianity has thus become a historic epoch in time. It is thus a thing in time, and not of the future world. But at times the author goes back to the very beginning, before Moses, and represents Christianity as being what Adam failed to secure. So regarded, Christianity is not a second half of the same period of time, but a new beginning. It thus marks the beginning of the future world. The author speaks of the great salvation of Christianity, which is so great because God has subjected the inhabited world to the rule of His people. This was the original goal of creation, but it was effected only in Christ. With Christ, therefore, we have a new creation.

Again, in 2:10 we read, "For it became him (God), for whom are all things, and through whom are all things, in bringing many sons unto glory, to make the author of their salvation perfect through sufferings." To subject the inhabited world to the rule of God's people was not too great a thing, if we remember that God created all these things, and that He Himself is the end of all. 2:14 again shows this. The atonement is usually represented in the terminology of cleansing. But here redemption is represented as the destruction of the devil and deliverance from death. Thus the idea is again carried back to Paradise, where man became subject to the devil and to death. In a similar way in chapter 4 Christianity is represented as a rest and a sabbath-keeping. This might have been used as a term referring to time, as expressing an *anapausis,* such as was the rest attained in Canaan. But Christianity is more than that. It is a *sabbath-keeping,* an actual realization of that which the sabbath signified at the creation. We are now living in the age of consummation and attainment.

## 2. The Typology of the Epistle

We shall now consider the relation between the content of the first *Diatheke* and that of the second. The relation is that the old prefigures the new. As to how the author conceives of this prefiguring, this is a rather difficult question. In 10:1 we read: "the law having a shadow (*skia*) of the good things to come, not the very image (*aute eikoon*) of the things. . . . " Thus we see that the law lacked something that we of the new covenant possess, namely *the very image.* But what does this expression mean? We might be inclined to say that the law had the shadow whereas we of today have the body. But the author does not say *body;* he says *image.* What kind of conception can it be that regards *image* and *shadow* as correlative terms?

There are two spheres in which such a conception is possible, namely the sphere of art and the sphere of philosophy. In art, the artist first makes a sketch, the *skia* (shadow), then he makes the picture, the *eikoon* (image). Similarly, the Old Testament might be said to possess only the preliminary outline or sketch, while the New Testament possesses the real picture. Considered in this way, both the sketch and the real picture are only *representations* of some real thing which lies beyond both of them. This real thing then would be *the heavenly reality.* This scheme may be represented by the following diagram:

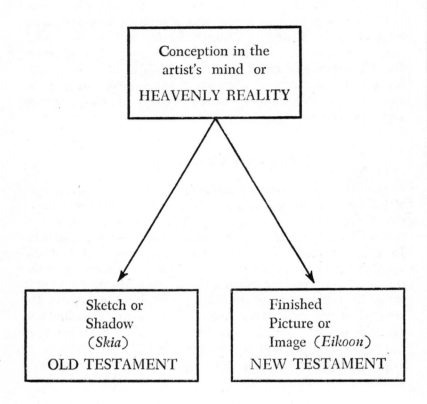

On the basis of the foregoing representation, both the Old Testament and the New Testament may be said to be derived from the Heavenly Reality, while in relation to each other, it may be said that the Old Testament prefigures the New.

The other, and more probable, although also more complicated and difficult, interpretation of the words is the philosophical one, which may be represented by the following diagram:

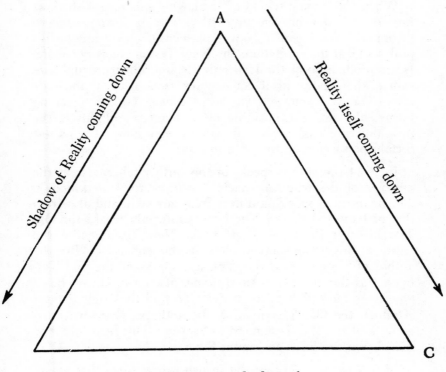

In the above diagram:

A represents the Heavenly Reality

B represents the Old Testament which is a "shadow" of the Heavenly Reality

C represents the New Testament which is the *substance* of the Heavenly Reality

B prefigures C because B is the "shadow" of A and C equals A

When the Epistle speaks of shadowing this means shadowing *down* (from heaven to earth), not shadowing *forward* (from Old Testament to New Testament). According to this philosophical interpretation, the New Testament is not merely a reproduction of the Heavenly Reality, but its actual *substance,* the Reality itself come down from heaven, the *aute eikoon* or very image. The word *eikoon,* besides meaning image, also had the meaning of *archetype,* and this is the meaning which precisely suits our purpose here. Let us test certain passages with this idea in mind.

In 9:24 the author speaks of the earthly tabernacle as the *antitype* of the true tabernacle (*antitupa toon alethinoon*). This manner of speaking differs from our own, and also from that of Paul and Peter. The latter uniformly regard the Old Testament as the type of which the New Testament is the antitype; this is the common New Testament usage. But the author of Hebrews, on the contrary, speaks of the Old Testament as the *antitype.* An antitype, of course, always has a type lying back of it as its model. To find the original *type,* of which the Old Testament is the antitype, then, we must go back of the Old Testament to heaven. This heavenly type was shown to Moses on Mount Sinai.

In 8:5 we are told that the Jewish priests serve that which is a copy and a shadow (*hupodeigma* and *skia*). The author adds that it is a copy and shadow *of the heavenly things.* Thus it is not a shadow projected or thrown forward (into the future), but a shadow cast down from heaven to earth. Moreover, the particular use made by the author of the adjective *true* (*alethinos*) ought to be noted. *Alethinos* is a much stronger word than *alethes* which is the more common word for *true. Alethinos* means not simply *the true,* but *the real, the genuine, the veritable.* It occurs elsewhere in the New Testament only in the Fourth Gospel. The *true* therefore is the real archetypal representation. So in the Fourth Gospel we read of *the true bread* coming down from heaven, and again of Christ as *the Truth* coming down from heaven.

This, then, is the one scheme of typology that is peculiar to this Epistle. The Epistle, however, also uses the ordinary conceptions of type and antitype as they are used by Peter and Paul. Thus in 9:8, with reference to the Holy of Holies, the author says that the fact that this was shut off to the people *pointed forward* to the fact that at a future time it would be opened to them. The Holy Spirit was signifying this, he says; therefore a *forecasting* was involved in this fact concerning the tabernacle. In 9:9 the author speaks of "a parable for the time then present." The Old Testament things, therefore, were a *parable;* that is, they were things called a parable in relation to the reality of the things of the New Testament. In 7:18 the author speaks of *a provisional commandment* contained in the Levitical priesthood. In Christ's own priesthood we have the subsequent and permanent commandment.

In the three cases cited above the author, while he does not actually use the terms *type* and *antitype,* nevertheless clearly shows a consciousness of the idea involved in those terms. There occur also a few instances in which the two representations are combined. The most striking of these is the reference to Melchizedek. The author states that Christ is a priest after the order (*kata ten taxin*) of Melchizedek. Thus he thinks of Melchizedek as the *model* and of Christ as the *copy.* The idea of temporal succession is also involved in this. Melchizedek is the type and Christ is the antitype. But then we read further of Melchizedek that he was *made like unto the Son of God* (*aphoomoioomenos*), a statement which introduces the other scheme, in which Melchizedek is regarded as the *antitype* back of whom lay the Son of God as the *type* or Heavenly Reality. Of that Heavenly Reality, Melchizedek is the *shadow* (*skia*). But now in the New Testament, when the Son of God as the Heavenly Reality has come down to this earth, Mechizedek comes to be regarded as the *foreshadowing* type of which Christ is the antitype.

The other instance in which these two modes of representation are brought together is found in the idea of *rest* (*anapausis*) in chapters 3 and 4. The New Testament rest had already been foreshadowed by the rest of Canaan in the Old Testament. But then the author goes on to speak of the higher, *heavenly* rest which through Christ has now come down to the readers — a rest of which the Old Testament rest in Canaan was in turn a *skia,* a shadow.

The figures most commonly used to represent the foreshadowing of the New Testament in the Old are drawn from the tabernacle ordinances, such as those of priesthood and sacrifice, in chapters 9 and 13. Christ is foreshadowed in the Old Testament, however, not only as priest, but also as king. This figure is brought out in Psalm 2:7, which is quoted in Heb. 1:5 and 5:5. The same idea is brought out in 2 Sam. 7:14 which is quoted in Heb. 1:5; and Psalm 40:7-9 which is quoted in Heb. 10:5. This is taken as spoken typically of Christ. We have here a confession of sin. It is David as king-priest who is here confessing sin, professing his readiness to do by obedience what the animal sacrifices could not acccomplish. There is a peculiar application of this Psalm, however. In the Psalm the true sacrifice lies in the internal sphere of obedience, not in the outward ceremony. The writer of Hebrews affirms that the vicarious sacrifice of Christ is a sacrifice of this type, being not external but internal.

Other instances of prefiguration, in which there is no specific office underlying the figure, are found in Psalm 22, which represents a righteous suffering saint. The author of Hebrews finds this Psalm fulfilled in Christ, and finds that through His salvation He becomes a source of salvation to others (2:12).

Another instance occurs in 2:13, where the writer quotes from Isaiah 8. Two statements from that chapter are quoted: (1) "I will put my trust in him"; (2) "Behold, I and the children whom God has given me." The author of Hebrews puts these words on the lips of Christ. This can only be explained on the principle that Isaiah, in his trust in God and in his identification with his children, *is a type of Christ.* Some interpreters, indeed, explain this merely as proof that any desirable quality or relationship found in the Old Testament characters may be applied to Christ. This is not the reason for the reference in Heb. 2:13, however. Isaiah in the chapter quoted from occupies a very critical position, and as such typifies the Messiah. The national hardening of the people had already begun in Isaiah's time, which was to have its culmination in the time of Christ. Thus we have before us one continuous process of hardening. And Isaiah, who lived at the time of the beginning of it, stands as the type of Christ who would live at the end of it. Now, it was due to this crisis that there was a separation effected. The prophet, in a sense, stood alone. Here, then, is the birth of the idea of a church within a church, the idea of *the invisible church*. This idea gave a new identification between the prophet and his most immediate circle, including his disciples, of whom we read. This identification extended not only to his disciples, of whom we read, but also to his children. These children were given him precisely for the express purpose of being identified with him in his trust in God. They were children of prophetic significance. Centuries later this was repeated, on a higher plane, in Christ. Again there was an unparalleled necessity for Christ to put his trust in God, and also there arose a close identification between Christ and the believers. This passage in Hebrews is unique in the Bible in speaking of believers as *children of Christ*. This expresses the closest identification possible.

There are also certain Old Testament statements of *Jehovah* which are in Hebrews referred to Christ, so that Jehovah becomes a type of Christ. These passages are Deut. 32:43, quoted in Heb. 1:6; Psalm 102:26-28, quoted in Heb. 1:12; Hab. 2:3, quoted in Heb. 10:37. From these references some again derive the interpretation that *everything* that is said of Jehovah in the Old Testament can properly be ascribed to Christ. The correct view, however, is that only the *eschatological* manifestations of Jehovah in the Old Testament may be referred to Christ. This is held also by Delitzsch. Only in these cases is Jehovah the type of Christ.

All the above are instances of prefiguration. In addition to these, however, there are also explicit predictions to be found.

There are especially three prophetic passages of the Old Testament that are favorites with the author of the Epistle to the Hebrews, namely Jer. 31:31, quoted in Heb. 8 and 10; Hag. 2:6, quoted in Heb. 12:26; and Psalm 45:7, 8, quoted in Heb. 1:8, 9.

The first passage is so plainly set forth as to require no special comment. The prophecy in Haggai speaks of a twofold shaking, one shaking lying in the past, referring to the giving of the law at Mount Sinai and the upheaval of the earth which accompanied it, and the other shaking still to take place in the future, a shaking far more comprehensive, including not only the earth but also the heaven. Now the author of the Epistle to the Hebrews finds in this a prediction of the introduction of the new covenant. (Whether he regarded the introduction of the covenant as lying in the past *for him* or as still in the future is not indicated; the full realization of it, at least, he thought of as still lying in the future.)

As to the third reference (Psalm 45:7, 8), there is a difference of opinion as to whether we have here a prediction or a prefiguration. The author quotes it in a way which allows two renderings. The one takes the term *God* as in the vocative case; then Christ is addressed as God. The other rendering takes *God* as in the nominative case, in which case we must translate "Thy throne *is* God" (verse 6). The same uncertainty occurs in the 7th verse: "Therefore God, thy God, hath anointed thee. . . " In the English versions the former of these, at least, is rendered as a vocative, making the divine name apply to Christ. And this is probably the correct rendering.

Now what is the author's view concerning the inferiority of the Old Testament as compared with the New Testament? Three elements may be gathered from the Epistle. These are expressed, first, in terms of place or sphere; second, in terms of substance or content; third, in terms of efficacy.

First, as to the inferiority due to place, the old covenant is terrestrial, earthly. It finds expression in terms of earth. The new covenant has its center in heaven and finds expression in heavenly forms. The priests in the former covenant were priests on the earth. Christ is a priest in heaven, indicating a difference not merely of location but also of importance. The Old Testament tabernacle was a sanctuary of this earth (9:1), a tabernacle of this creation. Therefore, according to 8:2 and 11:24, it was pitched by man and made with hands. This latter expression is also used by Paul to distinguish the earthly from the heavenly. This contrast is even applied to *revelation*: the one revelation is on the earth, the other is from heaven. The author represents God as giving oracles in two stages, the one on earth, and the other from heaven.

Second, as to the substance or content of the two dispensations, the author makes use of the contrast between flesh (*sarx*) and spirit (*pneuma*). The old covenant is spoken of as *sarkikos* and *sarkinos*. The second of these two terms is the strongest. *Sarkikos* means having the quality of *sarx*, or being *fleshly; sarkinos* means being composed of *sarx*, or being *fleshy*. The author speaks of *conscience* as the opposite of *sarkinos* or fleshy. Sometimes he also includes the idea of *spirit* as accompanying that of conscience.

The use of the term *sarx* here is quite distinct from that found in Paul's writings. The author of Hebrews says that the entire Old Testament is *sarx*. Paul, on the other hand, protests that the law is spiritual (*pneumatikos,* Rom. 7:14) and the commandment is holy, righteous and good. Paul used *sarx* with an ethical connotation of evil. But in Hebrews the term means simply *material* or *external.* Paul was also familiar with this same contrast, to be sure, but he expresses the contrast in other terms. He speaks of the Old Testament, for example, as "weak and beggarly elements," in contrast to the New Testament. He also speaks of the Old Testament law written on tables of stone, in contrast to the New Testament which has God's law written on tables of hearts of flesh. He speaks of circumcision of the *sarx,* that is, bodily circumcision, in contrast to the true circumcision which is that of the heart (Rom. 2:28, 29).

Another figure is found in Hebrews, namely that of the mountain (12:18). The Old Testament mountain is that which could be touched, that which was tangible and material. Over against this stands Mount Zion, the heavenly mountain. Also in 13:9 we read of *meats* in contrast with *grace*, and in 13:15 *animals* are contrasted with *the fruit of lips*.

Third, there is the contrast in point of efficacy. The same terminology is used here as in the case of flesh and spirit: the flesh is inert, but the spirit is dynamic. The clearest passage for this is 7:16. Here the author compares the two priesthoods, the Levitical priesthood and that of Christ. The Levites were made priests according to the law of a carnal commandment (*kata nomon entoles sarkines*), but Christ was made priest according to the power of an endless life (*kata dunamin zooes akatalutou*). The former was *legal* and therefore connected with the idea of inertia, as opposed to *kata dunamin* (according to power). It follows from this that the Levitical priesthood was a priesthood according to the law, which sprang from a commandment as its origin, which was a dead thing. Christ's priesthood, on the contrary, derived its dynamic character from a life-birth. Moreover, the two things are characterized as opposites in that the first was made by flesh, and was therefore transitory — something that must eventually decompose — whereas the life of Christ is indissoluble (*akatalutos*). Christ's priesthood is therefore eternal, having been tested by death and having passed through it unscathed.

This is taught in still another form, namely in that of the divine intention. The Old Testament law is dispensed with because of its weakness and unprofitableness. Its weakness is not merely a matter of degree, for in reality it accomplished nothing, since it made nothing perfect and did not lead to the goal. This is further implied in the quotation from Jer. 31:31, quoted in Heb. 8:8-12. The fathers did not continue in the covenant made with them. But in the new *Berith* the law would be put in their *minds* and written on their *hearts*. And the further promise is added: "Their sins will I remember no more." In both these respects, therefore, the Old Testament

law is inefficacious. In verse 7 the author goes on to say that God found fault with the first covenant, for otherwise there would have been no place found for a second.

3. The Problem of the Inferiority of the Old Testament from the Religious Point of View

The matters which we have been considering confront us with a serious problem: What value is still to be placed in such a weak system as the Old Testament is represented to be? Has the Old Testament not been proved to be altogether worthless? How could that which is called *flesh* make atonement at all and be the way to redemption?

The Pauline epistles also raise this problem. They speak of the inefficacy of the legal system. This is so emphasized as even to give the impression that the Old Testament was altogether devoid of grace. In this respect Paul's epistles go further than does the Epistle to the Hebrews. The reason for this is that Paul treats the law from the forensic point of view, and brings out that instead of leading to salvation the law brings a person under a curse. The Epistle to the Hebrews, on the other hand, regards the law as a system of atonement. The author's conclusion is purely a negative one, namely, that the law could not bring forgiveness. But in Paul's writings the law is represented as positively working *a curse*.

But how could a true religion exist under such a system at all? Several observations are in order. First, we may turn to the *types* of the Old Testament as something which should have led the people to something better. The author does not make much of this, however. The types were primarily for the people, but objectively they were for the mind of God. Nowhere in the Epistle has the author set himself really to solve the problem as stated above. Nor is it really solved in Paul's epistles.

Still there was a possibility of the significance of the sacrificial system entering into the subjective mind of the Old Testament believers, by the latter raising themselves to a higher state through the types. We see an indication of this possibility first at 10:3. In the Old Testament sacrifices there was a remembrance made of sin year by year. This was necessary, since it was impossible that the blood of bulls and goats could take away sins. This yearly practice was not intended merely for an objective purpose; it was a remembrance *in the minds of the people*. Because of this remembrance the Psalmist, in Psalm 40, was led to speak concerning sacrifices which *would* satisfy the will of God. It should be noted that it was *the Psalmist* who rose to this consciousness — an inspired writer, not an ordinary individual believer under the Old Testament. Still, he did write it, with the result that higher consciousness later became the common property of Old Testament believers. It was with the aid of *revelation*, therefore, that this higher consciousness was brought about.

Likewise Psalm 110 is quoted. Here we have the prophecy of a future Priest, after the order of Melchizedek. Thus there was the consciousness of a higher order of priesthood than the Levitical being possible, and there was the prophecy that at a future time such a higher priesthood would become actual.

Psalm 95 is also quoted, which speaks of the rest of Canaan. This idea of rest is eschatological, looking forward to the true rest which is to come in the future. The author of the Epistle to the Hebrews here again recognized, in one of the Old Testament Psalms, a certain higher consciousness on the part of the people of the Old Testament.

But the Old Testament consciousness, even without this spiritual understanding, could yet function with an absolute effect. The unbelievers of the Old Testament are referred to as being excluded not merely from the rest of Canaan, but also from the *absolute* rest, that is, from the *eternal* rest. This does not imply, of course, that the Old Testament unbelievers themselves realized or understood this. For them the proximate object was Canaan. Yet objectively they not only lost the inheritance of the earthly Canaan, but also were *eternally lost*, for God took their faith or unbelief in this proximate sense as having an eternal and final effect. For the *subjective* consciousness of believers there still *remained* an eternal rest — the heavenly rest which is the true rest of believers.

The Old Testament, however, had more than these mere symbols and ceremonies. It also contained direct *promises,* many of which were spiritual in content. And these promises were given repeatedly, from age to age. Therefore it was not necessary for the Old Testament believers to live exclusively on the basis of insight into the meaning of the types. Of these promises the author of Hebrews speaks much. Especially he speaks with reference to the divine promises made to the Patriarchs. He tells how they made the leap from the external to the internal and the spiritual. The Patriarchs even in their day saw the unnecessary character of the earthly Canaan, for they looked for the city which has foundations, whose builder and maker is God. Therefore they considered themselves strangers and pilgrims on this earth, even when they were living in the land of Canaan, the promised land. The author of the Epistle so interprets Gen. 23:4 and 47:9.

Finally, we must note the continuity of the Old Testament with the New. In 3:1-6 Moses is compared with Christ. There we read that Moses was *in* the house, whereas Christ is *over* the house. The implication is that the same house is meant in both cases, namely, God's house. (Compare Num. 12:17). In this house Moses is a servant, while Christ is a Son. The superiority of Christ to Moses is further brought out by the consideration that the builder of the house (Christ) is greater than the house and its contents (including Moses). Again the implication plainly is that the same house is meant, namely the house of which Moses was an inmate and in which he was a servant.

Christ is the *core* of the heavenly, spiritual world. Therefore *a real contact* existed between that world and the Old Testament house. The Old Testament house was therefore also in vital contact with the heavenly, spiritual reality.

In 11:26 we read that Moses preferred *the reproach of Christ* to the treasures of Egypt. This phrase, *the reproach of Christ,* is explained by its usage in 13:13, "Let us therefore

go forth unto him without the camp, bearing his reproach."
This reproach is thus seen to be a reproach which Christ
Himself first bore and which we now bear together with Him.
So we must similarly interpret the reproach of Christ borne
by Moses. This does not imply that Moses had a prophetic
knowledge of the sufferings of the future Messiah, but rather
that the reproach which Moses bore was objectively identical
with the reproach suffered by Christ and His people throughout the ages. This implies, therefore, that back of all the re-
proaches and sufferings which God's people have endured,
stood Christ. How this appeared to Moses' own subjective consciousness is told us in 11:25, "choosing rather to share ill
treatment with the people of God. . ."

### 4. The Epistle's Doctrine of Revelation: the Superiority of the New Revelation to the Old

The Epistle views religion as a product of revelation.
Thus it gives a warrant to speak of *revealed religion*. Revelation is a part of the supernaturalism of the Epistle. But there
is a special reason for the introduction of this idea here. The
author wanted to mark and compare progress in the matter
of revelation. This enables us to understand why he begins
abruptly with the discussion of his subject, omitting the for-
mality of an introduction. This interest is to be explained by
the intense concern of the writer with the subject of *the pro-
gressive character of revelation.*

A further reason for the author's stress on revelation as its
*Diatheke*-aspect, the concept of intercourse between God and
man. Revelation, therefore, is a conscious thing through and
through. Revelation is the speech of God to man. It forms
one side of the covenant intercourse, therefore. Note the
words used to express this intercourse of God with man. We
read that God *lalei* (talks), not that He *legei* (speaks). The
word used is suggestive of the kind of talk used in addressing
children, who cannot as yet understand ordinary adult speech.
The word brings out the practical intent of the speech.

The author speaks of *the word of God* in the singular, 4:12; 13:7. He also uses the expression *the word of hearing*, 4:2. He also speaks of *the oracles of God* (*logia tou Theou*), 5:12. The original meaning of *logia* is *little words*. How did this term get the meaning of *oracle?* When ancient people consulted an oracle they got in reply only mysterious or ambiguous phrases; hence *logia* came to have the meaning of *oracle,* and a divine origin was ascribed to them. Thus in Scripture the real word of God is called *the oracles of God.*

The author wanted the readers to be freed from their religious externalism. The word *speech* is more spiritual than anything else. It comes nearest to the spiritual and brings things in the inner spirit. In 6:1 the author speaks of *the doctrine of Christ* (*tou Christou logos*), meaning the word preached by Christ or the word bringing knowledge of Christ. Because it stresses the idea of revelation, the Epistle treats especially of the theological aspect of Christianity. It expresses a firm belief in the efficacy of *doctrine* as a means of grace. Paul as a rule first presents his argument as a whole, then proceeds to exhortation on the basis of the completed argument. But the author of Hebrews does not wait to finish his doctrinal argument, but immediately inserts hortatory material in the body of his doctrinal discussion. The writer was obviously a theologian before he wrote the Epistle; he had in mind a well defined doctrinal system. The author of Hebrews is not in this Epistle working out his doctrinal system for the first time, as Bruce wrongly supposes. Paul develops theology in his epistles, but only through woes and struggles. The author of Hebrews, on the contrary, writes very smoothly and evenly. He is obviously familiar with the ground he is traversing. In Hebrews doctrine is never introduced for its own sake; the theology of the Epistle is never of a merely speculative or scholastic type, although it does contain a pronounced intellectual vein, calling conversion, for example, *becoming enlightened.*

In agreement with this conception of revelation as a process of fellowship between God and man, the writer conceives of God as speaking through the Scripture: 4:12-14. He conceives of this as a continuous or permanent speech; God is *in His Word*, and this consideration leads the writer of the Epistle to personify the Word of God. He speaks of the Word judging, penetrating, etc. Such things could not be said of a word that stood by itself. After carrying out this personification, the author naturally returns to the idea of the speaking of God. Hence follows the identification of the Word with God.

Some have thought that the author's meaning is personal, that is, that *Logos* here means Christ. Although it is possible that the author was acquainted with Philo's idea of the term *Logos,* and that he conceived of it as John did, still this is not probable, because in that case the author would almost certainly have used the term *Logos* in the opening verses of the Epistle, where he speaks of the Son as being the effulgence of the Father's glory. The term *Logos* in the sense which it has in the prologue of the Fourth Gospel would almost certainly have been used in this connection by the author of Hebrews had he been familiar with that meaning of *Logos.* But as a matter of fact he does not use it in the opening verses of the Epistle where it would seem to fit so well.

Besides, it would hardly be necessary to affirm of Christ *that He is living,* which is what the author affirms of the Word of God in 4:12-14. The main point is that in this passage *the word* and *God* are identified. The word is like a two-edged sword. This is a figure of searching, which also contains the idea of judging. The revelation of God in Christ is both a searching and a judgment. It brings to light what is in a man. If unbelief is found in a man, he is searched and judged.

The first sentence of the Epistle (1:1-3) is carefully constructed. The unity and continuity of the old and the new revelation are strictly maintained. In both *God spoke.* The participle *having spoken* is a preparation for the finite verb *hath spoken.* The whole organism of revelation lies in these words. Whatever diversity may exist, still it is all a divine word. The responsibility of people under the New Testament may be greater, but this is not because the New Testament has more authority or more of God in it than the Old Testament has.

Over against the expression *of old time* stands the expression *the latter part of these days*. We have already explained this phrase. The Old Testament having been given *of old time*, it is related to the past; it came to a close with Malachi. This idea of finishing something also belongs to the other side of the comparison, for it inheres in the aorist *hath spoken* (*elalesen*). The writer lays stress upon the fact that God *has spoken* in Christ; both the old revelation and the new are accomplished facts.

The old revelation was made *to the fathers;* the new, *to us*. If the Epistle was originally intended for the use of Gentile Christians, the use of this expression *to the fathers* is interesting; it stresses the continuity of the new with the old.

The old revelation was *in the prophets;* the new is *in a Son*. This is the main difference between the two. Note that there is no possessive pronoun with *Son* in the original, nor any definite article. These were omitted with a purpose, so that the contrast to *in the prophets* is not *in His Son* nor *in the Son,* but rather *in a Son*.

In 7:28 we read that the law appoints men high priests, but the word of the oath, which was after the law, appoints a Son. It is a qualitative contrast; *a Son* is contrasted with *men*.

The old revelation was *in many portions,* for the prophets were many in number, but the new revelation possesses a unitary character. *In diverse manners* is an expression referring to the diverse mentality of the various prophets, and the various modes in which the revelation came to them; but in the case of the new revelation — the revelation made in Christ — the many modes are regarded as united or equalized in one.

Thus the author wishes to point out the inferiority of the old revelation in comparison with the new. In the new revelation all is simplified, and therefore superior. For in the case of that which comes in portions, each portion is necessarily incomplete. The synthesis of the New Testament is therefore superior to the revelation of the Old Testament. As a matter of fact, we find the synthesis of the Old Testament in the New Testament.

The question may be raised how far we can carry these modes in the Old Testament revelation. Precisely what is referred to by the words *in diverse manners?* Is the reference to various *modes of communication,* or is it perhaps to individual *collections* of the Old Testament revelations? As to the content or subject matter, we think of law, prophecy, wisdom and other kinds of Old Testament revelation. The expression *in the prophets* includes the definite article, therefore prophecy is here used in the widest sense, and covers all the prophets of the Old Testament. Is anything to be inferred from the word *in?* The Hebrew *Be* is rendered only inaccurately by the Greek *en,* since the Hebrew prefix does not have any local meaning, but simply means *through.* It is doubtful, however, whether such Hebraism can be discerned here, since elsewhere the author is careful with the Greek, as for example in 9:25, where the high priest is said to enter *in blood,* which in this case might mean *clothed in blood,* and need not mean *by means of blood.* Compare 1 John 5:6, "in the water and in the blood." There is some local significance here. In Heb. 11:2 the Greek *en* is used with a precise purpose. In 1:1 the word *dia* could not have been used because it would signify too little; it would mean that the prophets were mere mechanical instruments of revelation, an idea which the author clearly wished to avoid.

The opposite error is also guarded against, namely that of ascribing too much to the prophets, as if in the giving of the revelation only the first stage was directly under the control of God, but the delivering of the revelation to the people by the prophets was not under His control. By using the preposition *en* the author represents God as controlling both elements.

The explanation just presented may be correct, but it seems to overlook the meaning of the little word *en.* There is another possible explanation, which takes *en* in its full local sense, as in ,Matt. 10:20, "For it is not ye that speak, but the Spirit of your Father that speaketh in you." Here the preposition *en* has its local meaning: the Holy Spirit is actually *in* the speakers. Note also 2 Cor. 13:3, "a proof that Christ speaketh *in* me." To say that God was speaking in the prophets need not detract at all from their intelligence, but it does serve to emphasize the absolute character of the resultant prophecies. We need not be concerned so much about the *processes* of revelation, provided we maintain a firm conviction that the *product* of revelation is truly the infallible Word of God. This we find in Hebrews, which lays strong stress on the fact that the revelation was *in* the prophets.

Paul personifies the Scripture by using the expression *God says.* He does this only when quoting from statements of the Old Testament in which God is the speaker. Otherwise he says *Scripture said* or *as it is written.* But in the Epistle to the Hebrews God is everywhere represented as the speaker in the Old Testament. Only one passage, Heb. 4:7, names the human instrument, and even that one says *God saying in David.* The author goes so far as to say that it matters little who the human author may have been; the main thing is that God said it. Elsewhere he says, *Somewhere someone has testified.* Of course the author of Hebrews, thoroughly familiar with the Old Testament as he was, knew who that someone was, but still he does not name him.

We must now face the question, what idea does the author associate with the words *a Son.* It is a title given to Christ, to designate His superiority. The passages in which the term occurs are: 1:2, 5, 8; 3:6; 4:14; 5:5, 8; 6:6; 7:3, 28; 10:29. *Son of God* may be a Messianic title. The Son represents the Father, or the Son is the heir of the Father, or the Son is a recipient of the Father's love. Thus understood, the title *Son of God* ascribes to the Son a certain *function.*

But the term may also designate a *nature or origin*. In that case it is ontological rather than functional. If it is a Messianic title, then it has reference to the Messianic acts in history, referring to the presence of Christ on earth in the incarnate sphere. In this Messianic sense Christ could also be prophetically called the Son of God even before His incarnation. There is of course a certain sense in which the functional Messianic element existed before the incarnation; but broadly speaking, if we give it the functional sense, the meaning must be restricted to Christ's historical appearance in the world. If taken in the ontological sense, on the other hand, the title *Son of God* includes also Christ's pre-existence, without chronological limitations. Of course it must be borne in mind that the Messianic Sonship does not exclude the high ontological or eternal Sonship, nor did the latter render the former superfluous.

Turning now to the various passages, we shall begin with 1:3, 4. Here it is affirmed that Christ became "by so much better than the angels, as he hath inherited a more excellent name than they." Thus the measure of Christ's superiority to the angels is in the name which He inherited. The word *better*, of course, does not mean morally better; it is to be taken in the sense of superiority of nature. The name which made Christ superior to the angels was *Son of God*. The author illustrates this from the Old Testament: "For unto which of the angels said he at any time, Thou art my Son, this day have I begotten thee? and again, I will be to him a Father, and he shall be to me a Son?" This name of *Son* is said to have been *inherited* by Christ. This conception of inheriting places the matter within the sphere of time or history. There was a point of time at which He received the inheritance; therefore it appears that a functional or Messianic Sonship is referred to here. That is, Christ is said to be superior to the angels in so far as the Messiah is superior to the angels.

Now if we look at the second verse, we should have the presumption of a similar sense occurring there. Yet such would be a mistaken conclusion. For in the second of the two verses the Sonship is ontological. This is clear from the fact that the more excellent name is contrasted with the name of the angels. This comparison of Christ with the angels is one that is drawn out to some length through the chapter. The angels are contrasted with Christ in respect to their *nature*. Hence also Christ is referred to in respect to *His* nature. *God having spoken through a Son* omits the definite article. Therefore the term is generic, and does not refer to an office, but to His nature. If the reference were to His Messiahship, the definite article could not have been omitted. For *a* Messiah cannot be spoken of, since there can be *but one* Messiah; the form would have to be *the Messiah*, with the definite article. This indicates that the expression *in a Son* in verse 2 is generic. What follows in verse 3 reads like the unfolding of the conception of Sonship. Now the phrases *the effulgence of his glory, and the very image of his substance* are not functional phrases; rather, they describe what Christ is ontologically; they relate to His nature. But if these phrases relate to His nature, then the Sonship which is connected with them must also relate to His nature. So we conclude that the Sonship in verse 4 is functional, while that in verse 2 is ontological. But how can we reconcile these two in one and the same context?

The solution lies in verse 4, as to the manner in which the Messiah obtains the title. We read that He *inherited* the title. But such inheritance can only take place in the case of one who is already a Son by nature. Therefore the two senses are connected; because Christ is a Son ontologically, He is qualified to inherit the functional title of *Son* in the Messianic sense.

An objection may be raised that we are interpreting the word *inherited* in too literal a sense. In Greek to inherit sometimes has merely the meaning of *to obtain*. Thus the argument presented above would fall down. But in the passage under consideration the context seems to indicate the more specific meaning of inheriting, for in verse 2 it was stated that God had made His Son *heir* to all things; therefore the author had the literal meaning of *inherit* in mind. We conclude, then, that in this verse the word means not simply *obtaining,* but actually *inheriting.*

The next question we must consider is, how far does this ontological Sonship go? It dates back at least to the beginning of time. God has spoken in His Son, through whom also He made the worlds. But further it reached back of the creation into the sphere of absolute eternity, as is shown by the added phrases *the effulgence of his glory* and *the very image of his substance.* Therefore the term *Son* in the ontological sense describes not merely something that He *was,* but something that He *is,* throughout and beyond all time. Compare John 8:58, "Before Abraham was, I am."

In 1:8, "thy throne, O God, is for ever and ever," something may be said in favor of the ontological interpretation of *Son* in the first phrase of the verse. The Son is here addressed *as God,* although Westcott and Hort suggest the rendering *thy throne is God,* taking *ho Theos* not as a vocative but as a predicate nominative. According to this interpretation the Son is affirmed to sit as it were on the shoulders of God. But in the margin Westcott and Hort remind us of the other rendering. If we follow their preferred rendering, the conception of sonship involved is a high one, but does not necessarily pass beyond the functional conception. In that case the scepter spoken of would be a scepter of kingship, but not of Deity. And the kingship is traced to the Anointed One as on the seat. The other rendering (*thy throne, O God. . . .*) however can only be ontological. Therefore the question depends on the original author's meaning.

In 3:6 we have the contrast between Christ and Moses. The contrast is in the sphere of office and function. The superiority of Christ is again connected with His being *Son.* Moses was faithful as a servant, but Christ was faithful as a Son. Further, Moses was faithful *in* the house, because he was a servant; but Christ was faithful *over* the house, because He was a Son.

This is explained from the Messianic conception of Sonship. Christ had perfect supervision over the house. The thought, it should be carefully noted, is not that Moses was over the Old Testament house and Christ is over the New Testament house, but rather that Christ is a Son over *the same* house in which Moses was a servant. Christ was also the Messianic Son, and therefore, in the time of Moses, it was Christ that built the house. Hence His Messianic Sonship goes back of His incarnation and reaches back into the historical pre-existence.

In verse 4 we read, "he that built all things is God." Does this mean that Christ is a builder, but that there exists also a greater builder, namely God? If that is the meaning, then the text contains a mark of difference between God and the Son, thus representing God as being more than the Messiah. But another exegesis refers the words *he that built all things is God* also to Christ, so that the statement amounts to a climax in the magnifying of Christ. He that builds is God, but it is Christ, the Son, who builds; therefore in this text Christ is called God Himself. If this exegesis is correct, then the title *Son* cannot here be restricted to the functional level; the two senses would coalesce. But which is really the correct interpretation is not certain.

In 4:14 the author's conception of Sonship is a very high one. He gives exceptionally high value to the high priesthood of Christ, and derives its eminence from the Sonship. The Messianic Sonship in itself may be sufficient for that.

In 5:5 the author again speaks of the priesthood of Christ, stating that He did not usurp it, but was called to it by God. So Christ also glorified not Himself to be a high priest, but He that spake unto Him, *Thou art my Son.* The God who said to Him *Thou art my Son* is the one who made Him priest. According to some interpreters this means: "But God, *when* he spake to him," instead of *that* He spoke to Him. This interpretation would make the Sonship functional. The speaking amounted to making Him priest. This is hardly plausible, though, because nowhere does the author identify the Messiahship and the priesthood.

In 7:28 we read that the law appoints men high priests, but the word of the oath appoints a Son, who is a Son before He is made high priest. Hence Christ did not glorify Himself to be made high priest, but God gave this office to Him because He had the Sonship forever, that is, He was Son forever before becoming high priest as Messiah. Thus there exists not an identity but a *congruity* between the two offices of high priest and Messiah. The office of priesthood thus comes to Him from the same source as being called *Son*. This would seem to indicate a Messianic Sonship; but in 7:28 the ontological Sonship seems clearly implied, since the appointment to the priesthood comes as an acknowledgment of the Sonship.

In 7:28 *a Son* is contrasted with *men,* which confirms the idea that the eternal or ontological Sonship must be meant here. The Sonship of Christ, therefore, in the *deepest* sense is the ontological divine Sonship, which lies back of the Messianic Sonship.

6:6 and 10:29 yield us nothing new. These passages imply the terrible character of the sin of those who have crucified and trodden underfoot the Son of God. Thus they imply a very high standing of the Son. Still, the Messianic Sonship would be quite sufficient for this. In 7:3 we read that Melchizedek was made like into the Son of God, which is a reversal of the usual statement, that Christ was made a priest after the order of Melchizedek. The statement that Melchizedek was made like unto the Son of God has been understood as an *anticipation* of the Son of God afterwards to come, the Messiah. While this interpretation would be possible in itself, the context forbids it in this case. Note the point of the comparison: Melchizedek and Christ are compared with respect to their *eternity.* What kind of an eternity is this? Does it extend only forward, or also backward? If the former, then the Messianic sense is sufficient, and the interpretation of anticipation can be accepted as the correct one. But

Melchizedek is called eternal in both directions, since it is affirmed of him that he is without father, without mother, without genealogy, having neither beginning of days nor end of life, and that therefore he is like unto the Son of God. So we must conclude that in this verse the Son is ontologically spoken of.

A point of interest here is the question of how the idea of Sonship in both senses contributes to the superiority of the new revelation over the old. As Messianic Son, Christ is *the ideal Revealer*. The Messiahship is the ideal position, high above all the prophets of the Old Testament. In harmony with this, the revelation referred to in connection with the Son is a revelation of *speech*. He who holds the highest office brings also the highest message. But apart from this, it is also true that the ontological Sonship has a bearing on the superiority of the new revelation, as seen in the comparison made between Christ and the angels. This is an ontological comparison, not merely a comparison of height of position. Note the traits brought out with respect to the angels: they are made winds, and flames of fire; still they are under time, and are subject to change; the Son is not so, however: for His nature is superior to theirs. This superiority of nature makes Christ's revelation also superior in nature, character and person. The new revelation is thus marked by what Christ *is*, as well as by what He says. This idea is also worked out in the Fourth Gospel. Here in Hebrews it is further confirmed that we are to think of the superiority of the new revelation because of what Christ *is*, in that His likeness to God and His close connection with God are brought out.

Further there are two terms which require discussion, found in 1:3, *the effulgence of his glory* (*apaugasma*) and *the very image of his substance* (*charakter*). Two questions should be asked regarding these terms: (1) What figure of speech is involved in each? (2) For what purpose are these figures employed? In answer to the second question we might say that these figures are employed for a Trinitarian theological construction, representing the second Person as the effulgence of the glory, etc., of the first Person of the Trinity. Or we might say that these figures are employed for a cosmical representation, to show how the glory of God is carried into the world of creation. In the latter case the figures would be *economic* phrases, expressing the relation between God and the world.

First, then, we inquire what are the figures of speech in 1:3. The first word concerned, *apaugasma,* is from the verb *apaugazein,* meaning *to shine before.* Note that the noun ends in *-ma,* to distinguish it from the noun ending in *-mos.* Nouns ending in *-ma* denote the *product,* whereas those ending in *-mos* denote the *process* itself. Here we have the concrete product of the act, not the abstract act itself. The Son, therefore, is the product of an act of shining forth in God. He is the product of the radiation of God. The word, however, can mean *refulgence* as well as *effulgence;* that is, it can mean a shining back, an effulgence that has become separated from its source, like a moon that is a replica of another moon, instead of an effulgence such as the mere tail of a comet, for instance. The difference between the two is that *refulgence* would place the emphasis on the distinct personal existence of the Son. The choice between *effulgence* and *refulgence* as a translation of *apaugasma* is indifferent so far as the question of whether the term in 1:3 is theological or cosmical in meaning is concerned. If it is used in a theological sense, then the *effulgence* would refer to the eternal generation of the Son from the Father; or if we prefer to translate *apaugasma* by *refulgence,* then the theological usage of the term would serve to mark the Son as a separate person in the divine Trinity. But if the usage is cosmical, then Christ's *effulgence* would mean that Christ is carrying the glory of God into the world, yet never being detached from God. And if we render *apaugasma* by *refulgence,* the cosmical usage would mean that Christ is immanent in the world, duplicating the glory of God in the world.

With respect to the term *charakter,* again two interpretations are possible, each of them going, however, with one of the two possible interpretations of *apaugasma,* namely trin- itarian or cosmical. *Charakter* comes from the verb *charas- sein,* meaning *to scratch.* The noun can be either active or passive in meaning. Used actively, it means *a designer* or *an engraver,* and with respect to Christ, *he who engraves.* This would be equivalent to the active participle *ho charassoon.* But passively the word means *he who is engraved upon,* equiv- alent to the perfect passive participle *ho kecharagmenos.* Now, the passive rendering involves the trinitarian interpretation, whereas the active sense involves the cosmical interpretation. In Greek the word was used with reference to *a seal.* In the active sense it meant the lines on the bottom of the seal which made the impression. But in the passive sense it meant the character or impression that was made. So Christ either rep- resents the character *on* the seal of God, or else His is the image *made with the seal,* that is, God's stamp is placed upon the Son so that He as second Person of the Trinity becomes the impression of the first Person, being the character *from* the seal.

With regard to the question of deciding between the ren- derings *effulgence* and *refulgence,* the church fathers uni- formly rendered it by *effulgence.* But over against them stand Philo and the earlier Wisdom literature. In Philo the word meant sometimes the one and sometimes the other. In one passage also his meaning is uncertain, presenting the same difficulty as we face in Heb. 1:3. In the *Wisdom of Solomon* 7:26 the same uncertainty occurs. We may observe, how- ever, that of the four passages involved in Philo only one re- quires the rendering *refulgence,* while the other three require *effulgence.* The rendering *effulgence* thus has the stronger support.

With regard to the meaning of *charakter* the same uncer- tainty exists. If we could have certainty concerning the mean- ing of this word, it would be possible to decide at once whether the former term (*apaugasma*) is to be interpreted theologi- cally or cosmically. Now Philo says: "the Logos is the char- acter *of* the seal of God." Thus in this instance he takes it actively. The context shows that he has in mind the Logos as an instrument with which God makes an impression on the world. The soul is stamped with this seal. But he also uses it passively, when he says: "The spirit of man is a character of the divine power." Thus we are again left in uncertainty.

How shall we decide whether to adopt the trinitarian or the cosmical interpretation? The probability is in favor of the former. This is also the traditional interpretation. Only in some modern theological writers is the cosmical interpretation favored. Bruce seems to prefer the latter, though he does not expressly say so. In favor of the cosmical interpretation it might be argued that in verse 2b the greatness of the Son is described from the point of view of His relation to the world. We should also note that in verse 3b we again have a cosmological statement (*upholding all things by the word of his power*). Therefore we might expect that the cosmical interpretation is to be preferred in the intervening clause also. But the arguments for the theological or trinitarian interpretation outweigh this consideration: (1) The author speaks in terms of *being*, not in terms of the Son's *doing*; (2) the words are more naturally construed in the theological sense, since the world is not mentioned here; (3) the Son is called *the character of the divine substance;* to take this cosmically would imply a communicating of the divine substance to the world, which is too pantheistic a conception to be consistent with the rest of the Epistle. The theological or trinitarian interpretation, on the other hand, results in no such difficulty.

One more observation may be made: if we accept the cosmical interpretation, we still cannot get rid of the theological background. We must still ask, why is the Son a fitting image to act as seal for the world? The theological idea is a necessary implication in the background, even if we accept the cosmical interpretation.

With regard to the relation of the two phrases to each other, if we take them in the trinitarian theological sense, then the first phrase expresses the essential unity of the Godhead by reason of the identity of the Father and the Son; we cannot think of the Son without the Father; and the second phrase emphasizes the result, namely, the *likeness* of the Son to the Father. . In theological language, then, the expression *the effulgence of his glory* assures us of the Son's being *homoousios* with the Father, and the expression *the very image of his substance* assures us of the Son's being the *monogenes* of the Father.

The third verse contains one more statement which adds to the foregoing the idea of the superiority of Christ: *upholding all things by the word of his power.* Here the word is represented as being Christ's *possession.* Therefore in this text Christ is not represented as Himself being the word. Note the connection with the preceding clause by means of the particle *te*: "*and so* upholding all things by the word of his power." What he upholds is *ta panta*, which is not the same as simply *panta.* The latter means simply numerically *all things,* whereas the former means *the universe.* In John 1:2 we read simply *panta*, meaning *all things.* But not so here in Heb. 1:3, where we have *ta panta.* Therefore we must understand the verb *pheroo* as indicating something more than mere sustentation. It also includes a leading and guiding of the world to its appointed goal. Christ is therefore represented as the *Author of providence* in the broadest sense. To say that He does this *by the word of His power* amounts to an attestation of His *divine* power. This expression *by the word of his power* is not a Hebraism, as if meaning simply *by his powerful word,* which in the context would have the effect of an anticlimax. Moreover it is not the habit of the author of the Epistle to use Hebraisms.

Note, in conclusion, the whole general comparison in chapter 1 between Christ and the angels. The angels are not compared with Christ merely as exalted creatures, but also as revealers and administrators, in which respects also Christ is superior to them. Therefore the author's conclusion at the end of the passage (2:2) is to the effect that if the word spoken by angels is great, how much greater must be the word spoken by Christ. The word spoken through the angels is the word of *the law*. There are two other passages referring to this in the New Testament. One of these is Acts 7:35, spoken by Stephen: "Ye who received the law as it was ordained by angels. . ."; the other is Gal. 3:19, "it was ordained through angels by the hand of a mediator."

The Old Testament basis for this conception is found in two passages, Deut. 33:2 and Psalm 68:17. The former of these is highly poetical language: "Jehovah came from Sinai. . . And he came from the ten thousands of holy ones: At his right hand was a fiery law for them." The second passage is also highly poetical: "The chariots of God are twenty thousand, even thousands upon thousands: the Lord is among them, as in Sinai, in the sanctuary." Compare the LXX renderings of these two passages.

The New Testament passages cited above are not of an argumentative character at all; the doctrine involved in them is rather represented as a generally accepted one. Therefore we must regard it as current doctrine at the time of writing. But it could hardly have been developed merely out of the Old Testament passages just cited. And yet it appears that the doctrine of the connection of the angels with the giving of the law was well known. This is also corroborated by Josephus, who represents Herod as saying that the Jews had learned the holiest of laws from God through angels, Ant. XV, chap. 5, par. 3.

As to the motive of this doctrine, we may say that the proximate motive was to keep God from too close and direct contact with the world, that is, to preserve the majesty of God. With Paul in Galatians the motive is quite a different one, however; he makes a distinction between the angels and God in the importance of the dispensation of revelation: God gave *the promise,* not through angels, but *directly;* the law, however, was *indirectly* given through Moses and the angels. What is given most directly stands as the highest revelation Therefore the promises stand higher than the law. In the case of Stephen's words we have again a different motive for attributing to the angels a connection with the giving of the law. Stephen *exalts* the law by referring to it as an ordinance given through angels.

The passage in Hebrews is parallel to the Pauline representation. The law, as given through angels, imposes a lesser responsibility than does the revealing word of the Son. Of course this does not mean that the word given through angels is less true or less reliable, for in the ultimate analysis it is just as much the Word of God as the word given through the Son. The word given through angels also *proved stedfast* (2:2). Then why is the responsibility greater in the case of the word given by the Son? Because of the *more direct* revelation; the greater the impression of the majesty of God, the greater is the transgression involved in disobedience. It is interesting to observe that the author does not answer the possible objection of an indirectness remaining still because the revelation is through the Son. This shows that the author did not look upon Christ as an intermediate being, but as Himself truly divine.

This whole idea of the angels being involved in the giving of the law has been brought into connection with Paul's statement that the entire Old Testament stood under *the rudiments of the world* (*stoicheia tou kosmou*), Gal. 4:3, 9. These rudiments are characterized as weak and poor. Paul uses the word again in Col. 2:20, "If ye died with Christ from the rudiments of the world, why, as though living in the world, do ye subject yourselves to ordinances. . . ?" Some modern expositors have taken *stoicheia* as referring to angels. It must be admitted that the word does sometimes have this meaning in the Greek. It is derived fom the verb *stoichein*, meaning *to step*. The primary meaning of the noun, therefore, is *steps*. Further it means *fence pickets* (as parts making a fence), *component elements, the letters of the alphabet* (as component parts of words), *elements of things* (hence physical elements), *elements in heaven* (the stars), and finally *the angels* (an extreme form of the belief being that angels dwelt in stars as their physical bodies).

The last mentioned idea gained some prevalence even among the Jews. Therefore there is a possibility that Paul made use of this word in referring to angels at times, to bring out the idea of the intimate connection of the angels with the physical world. And it is just this that Paul sought to bring out in the passage referred to (Col. 2:20), namely the physical constitution of the ancient stage of the religion of the people of Israel. He even goes so far as to identify this feature of their religion with a similar feature in pagan religion. The Jewish religion, as a religion of ceremonies, shared some features of pagan religion. Of course in the matter of origin the two are essentially different, but from a formal point of view there are resemblances. Can we, then, with this consideration in mind, admit that the idea of angels is implied in Col. 2:20, as suggested above? We have seen the reasons given by the author of Hebrews for the inferiority of the Old Testament. The chief reason was the external and material (*sarkikos*) element involved in it. Possibly, therefore, the author also introduces the idea of angels as associated with the external physical administration. Compare Robertson Smith in *The Expositor*, 1881, pp. 38 ff.

The other passage in which this superiority of the revelation through Christ is brought out is Heb. 12:25: "See that ye refuse not him that speaketh. For if they escaped not when they refused him that warned them on earth, much more shall not we escape who turn away from him that warneth from heaven (that gave oracles from heaven)." Here again the emphasis is on the greater responsibility under the New Testament. Again the difference is that the one revelation is given on earth, and the other revelation is from heaven. Note also the context which follows: "whose voice then shook *the earth. . .*"

Why should the giving of the law at Sinai be referred to as an oracle *on earth?* Because it came from the mountain, which is in keeping with the entire representation of a terrestrial dispensation. But then how can the revelation through Christ be regarded as exclusively a heavenly revelation? Because the author represents Christ as a portion of heaven come down to earth. In His voice we hear a heavenly voice, not a voice of earth.

This is further worked out in tracing the difference in the *effect* of the two revelations. The first had an *earthly* effect, whereas the second has a more *universal* and *permanent* effect. In the former only the earth was shaken; but as to the latter, the author quotes a promise given in Haggai that yet a little while and there will be a shaking that will include the heaven as well as the earth. This promise in Haggai speaks of the revelation through Christ. Note that the author lays great stress on the words· *yet once more;* the shaking is one that cannot be repeated; it is the final shaking, and therefore it represents the final transformation of the whole world or universe. The author further says that this final shaking signifies the passing away of all things *that were made* and therefore can be shaken, in order that the things which *cannot be shaken* may remain.

# The Priesthood of Christ in the Epistle to the Hebrews

# CHAPTER IV

## THE PRIESTHOOD OF CHRIST IN THE EPISTLE TO THE HEBREWS

The priestly office of Christ stands side by side with His revealing function. In one passage the author connects all three offices of Christ, referring to them in order (1:1-3). But especially the revealing function and the priesthood are conjoined in 3:1, "Consider the Apostle and High Priest of our profession, Christ Jesus." Note that the single definite article is used for both nouns, binding the two closely together. Also note that the author says *consider* the Apostle, etc. Christ is worthy of attention in both of these capacities, as is indicated by the added words *of our confession (profession)*. This, then, is what we must confess of Christ. Further, the *goal* is stated: *partakers of the heavenly calling, consider* . . . . To reach this heavenly calling, we must consider Christ.

The Epistle to the Hebrews stands alone among the New Testament books in calling Christ priest. Still there are sufficient analogies for this in the contemporary literature. In the Talmud mention is made of the *heavenly altar*. The one that officiates at the altar is called the *Metaphroon*. We also read: "The Messiah is dearer to God than Aaron." In the Targum the Messiah is represented as "making intercession for the sins of the people," a paraphrase of Isa. 53:12. Philo in speaking of the Logos calls Him High Priest, and speaks of Him as great and sinless. He also speaks of His mildness and benevolence. He also says that Melchizedek was His type, and he ascribes to Him various priestly functions.

Still there is a difference between Philo's conception and that of the Epistle to the Hebrews, for the former is characterized by a total absence of soteric elements; in it the Logos plays no expiatory part. Philo's interest is solely in two things: cosmical speculation, and spiritualizing. These two motives control his entire representation. Moreover Philo asserts that the sanctuary of the Logos is *the cosmos of the soul*, whereas the Epistle to the Hebrews represents it as a reality existing in heaven. What does Philo mean by saying that the sanctuary of the Logos is the cosmos of the soul? He regards the Logos as standing metaphysically between God and the world, bringing order into the cosmos and reason into what was a chaos. In the soul, Philo regards the Logos as the spiritualizing element. But he never regards the Logos as an expiating element; rather, he regards the Logos as a divider separating evil from good.

·The *Testament of the Twelve Patriarchs* contains a prediction about the priest-king who is at the same time to be also a prophet. Various acts are ascribed to him, mostly eschatological in character. He is also brought into connection with Abraham. The passage is based on Psalm 110. It is said of him that he shall have no successor in eternity, that sin shall disappear, etc. Compare the *Testament of Levi,* chapters 8 and 18. Note that here the priesthood is derived from the tribe of Levi, and that no expiatory function is ascribed to the priest. The Epistle to the Hebrews, on the other hand, emphasizes the derivation of the High Priest from the tribe, not of Levi, but of *Judah* (7:14).

To explain the absence of the term *priest* in reference to Christ from the New Testament outside of Hebrews, we may say that there was less need for it, since the sacrificial character of Christ's work was universally recognized. In Isa. 53 we find mention of *the Servant of Jehovah,* who is represented as the sacrificial lamb; yet the idea is also expressed that he actually and freely surrenders himself to this end. Therefore the idea of priesthood is strongly brought out. Christ Himself interprets the 110th Psalm messianically, thus clearly implying the priestly function.

We might refer to the passage in Zech. 6:12,13, ". . . and he shall be a priest upon his throne." But no trace of this is found in the New Testament. John the Baptist made use of Isa. 53, however. Christ Himself never calls Himself *priest,* but He does represent Himself as the *sacrifice* in the establishment of the new covenant. Neither does Paul call Christ *priest,* but he does use various forms of expression which imply the idea of priesthood. He speaks of Christ as the *sacrifice,* the *mercy-seat,* as *giving Himself up for us,* as *an offering and sacrifice to God.*

For 1 Tim. 2:5 we find the closest approach to the priestly idea: "For there is one God, one mediator also between God and men, himself man, Christ Jesus." Verse 6 continues, "who gave himself a ransom for all. . ." Note also Rom. 8:34, "It is Christ Jesus that died, yea rather, that was raised from the dead, who is at the right hand of God, who also maketh intercession for us."

In John's epistles Christ's sacrificial death is referred to John's closest approach to the idea of priesthood is found in the idea of the *Paraclete.* This term is to be understood as meaning not merely *a comforter* but also *an advocate.* In the Book of Revelation, believers are represented as being made kings and priests unto God (Rev. 1:6); therefore Christ in making us such, must also be such Himself; compare Rev. 5:10; 20:6.

In Peter's epistles believers are called *a holy priesthood* to offer up spiritual sacrifices *through Christ.* Therefore Christ must also be a priest. Neither Peter's epistles nor the Book of Revelation stress the *uniqueness* of Christ's priestly office, however, since they speak of that which believers share in common with Christ.

Two passages in Acts employ the term *archegos.* In Acts 3:15 Christ is called *the prince of life,* and in 5:31 He is called *a Prince and a Saviour.* Even though it is true that Hebrews is the only New Testament book that actually calls Christ *priest,* still this idea is not presented in Hebrews as if it were a novelty, but rather as a well known idea, as is evident from the manner in which it is introduced, 3:1.

The priestly title given Christ in Hebrews is both that of *High Priest* and that of *priest*. Some hold that these two terms are used indiscriminately by the author. This however is not the case. When Psalm 110 is quoted, it is necessary to speak of Christ as *priest*, with reference to Melchizedek. Only in one passage, 5:10, is the quotation from Psalm 110 given more freely: here He is called *high priest*, but this may be explained by the context; the reference is a prelude to the subsequent argument. In that argument Christ is contrasted both with Melchizedek and with Aaron. Where a comparison with Aaron is expressed or implied, Christ is called *High Priest* (2:17; 4:14; 5:1; 7:26, 28; 8:13; 9:11, 12). When the comparison is between Christ and the Levitical order, He is called *priest*. In one passage where we would expect the term *High Priest* the term *priest* occurs (10:21, incorrectly translated *high priest* in the Authorized Version). In this text the term *priest* is explained by the accompanying adjective *great*, the expression *great priest* being really equivalent to *high priest*. 9:6, 7 shows clearly that the terms *priest* and *high priest* are not indiscriminately used. The author was quite conscious of the distinction between them.

What is the essence of the office of priest? A priest is one who brings near to God. His function differs from that of a prophet in that the prophet moves from God toward man, whereas the priest moves from man toward God. This idea is found in 5:1, where the author gives a quasi-definition of a priest: "For every high priest, being taken from among men, is appointed for men in things pertaining to God, that he may offer both gifts and sacrifices for sins." Thus a priest is one who brings men near to God, who leads them into the presence of God.

This conception must be closely defined, however. The priest does not merely *send*, but actually *brings* men near to God. Other elements must therefore be added to the idea. The priest himself must approach God first. Therefore the representative element must be included in the conception;

the priest brings men to God representatively, through himself. Secondly, in the priest, the nearness to God is not merely *counted* as having taken place for the believers, as a mere *imputation*. Rather, so close is the connection between the priest and the believers that a contact with God on his part at once involves also a contact with God for them. The contact with God is passed on to them as an electric current through a wire. Thirdly, a priest does not content himself with establishing contact only at one point; he draws the believers after himself, so that they come where he is.

It is plain that to satisfy these requirements there must be a close identification between the priest and his followers. The line must be unbroken. They must follow him in his nature. All of this may be embodied in the term *identification*. That is the great prerequisite. Note here the emphasis on *the two natures* of Christ. As revealer, Christ's divine nature is emphasized, 1:3. But in the priesthood, the emphasis is on His human nature. If He had been an angel, He could not have been a priest. This was different from the Jewish tendency, which was toward a separation between God and man and which therefore represented *an angel* as ministering at the altar. This is a striking difference.

This idea is dwelt upon in various passages. In 5:1 the human nature is emphasized. The direction is toward God. Note the use of the present participle, not the aorist: *being taken from among men*. This is significant, as indicating a present requirement. Otherwise He could not function as a priest.

In 2:10ff. we note the steps in which this close identification between Christ and His people is worked out. The new covenant is made subject not to angels but to man. The author quotes the 8th Psalm in this connection, which speak of man's calling at his creation. From this the author takes occasion to say that this calling is first realized in Christ. Christ bears rule over the whole world *for us*. Christ and His people are therefore identified here. This is the first step in the bringing out of this identification.

Secondly, Christ is called *the captain of our salvation* (*archegos soterias*). In one other place in the Epistle Christ is called *archegos* (*archegos pisteoos*, 12:2). The word *archegos* is compounded from *arche* and *ago*, and therefore signifies *one who leads at the beginning or head*. It also means *author*, as the *one who finishes*. In Acts the term is translated *prince*, but might equally well be rendered *leader*, since *Prince of life* clearly means *the Captain of our life;* He is the first to inherit it in His person as the life which the others shall later be made to share. This is also very likely the meaning of the term in the phrase *Prince and Saviour*, that is, *leader of salvation*. So also in Heb. 12:2, Christ is the *leader* or *captain* and perfecter of our faith. In 2:10 the idea is especially prominent, however. Christ draws us after Himself to salvation. He led the way to glory.

With respect to the third step, the author, while not using the term *priesthood* in the passage 2:10 ff., nevertheless clearly implies it in the idea expressed in verse 11, "For both he that sanctifieth and they that are sanctified are all of one: for which cause he is not ashamed to call them brethren." This gives us a substitution of a distinctly priestly idea for the idea of captainship in the preceding verse. We have here a very strong identification between Christ and the believer, an identification in point of origin. This does not mean physical origin of descent, as of Adam or Abraham; the author's proof speaks purely of spiritual relations, quoting Psalm 22 and Isa. 8. It is a oneness in the spiritual sphere and in the exercise of faith. He is father and they are children. They are spiritual brethren. The oneness is a oneness in relation to God, as a covenant standing.

In the fourth step this oneness is still further worked out. Since those who are regarded as children of Christ are partakers of flesh and blood, He also partook of the same; He also enters upon a physical unity with them, by His incarnation.

Finally, as a fifth step, Christ is represented as becoming one with His people in all their *experience*: "it behooved him in all things to be made like unto his brethren" (2:17). All this qualifies Him for the priesthood, in order that "he might become a merciful and faithful high priest in things pertaining to God."

Defining the priesthood in this way does not *necessarily* involve connecting it with sin and redemption. Even in a sinless state a priestly head might be conceived of. Yet the author nowhere reflects on this abstract possibility. As a matter of fact he always links up the priesthood with the ideas of sin and redemption from sin. He might have omitted this and followed Philo in the latter's abstract representation. There are indeed some scholars who do attribute such a representation to the author of Hebrews, alleging that the author regards sin and redemption merely as an incidental episode. According to this view, Christ was priest before the entrance of sin, and will remain priest after the removal of sin. Dr. Abraham Kuyper, among others, held this view of the matter, finding the central point in the comparison of Christ with Melchizedek, an eternal priest. Dr. Kuyper, however, held that the *incarnation*, in distinction from the priesthood, is wholly the result of sin and redemption. He held, however, that even in a sinless universe Christ would have been an unincarnate priest, being such from all eternity. This view involves an inconsistency, however, in that Kuyper maintains a persistence of Christ's human nature after His ascension (as orthodox Christology in general maintains), so that *now*, at any rate, Christ's priesthood cannot be regarded as separate from His incarnation.

Westcott also holds this idea. Although less orthodox with regard to the rest of Scripture, he remains closely in touch with the teaching of the Epistle to the Hebrews. Westcott rightly conceived of the priesthood and the incarnation as going together. Hence he also holds that there would have been an incarnation even if the human race had never fallen into sin.

Kuyper's reference to Melchizedek to substantiate his view of an eternal priesthood apart from sin and redemption is very weak, since it is a fact that Melchizedek was a priest *after* the entrance of sin into the world.

Westcott quotes certain passages in favor of his view, as follows: 1:2, ". . . his Son, whom he appointed heir of all things, through whom also he made the worlds." Westcott argues that here the Son is represented as becoming heir of all things because all things were made through Him, not as a result of sin and redemption, but because of His work at the creation. But we may interpret the verse more accurately as follows: "He made him *redemptive* heir of all things, as he had also created all things through him." Because He was the Creator of all things, Christ was also appointed redemptive heir of all. Without the fact of sin, therefore, there would have been no appointment to heirship. Moreover, this passage does not speak of the priesthood at all, so we may conclude that Westcott makes too much of it. Nor is the incarnation mentioned in this passage; the inheritance could also have taken place without the incarnation.

2:5 ff. shows that the human race had its destiny set for it at the creation. This was not fulfilled in humanity itself, but it was fulfilled in Christ. Westcott therefore argues that even apart from sin and redemption, Christ's incarnation would have been necessary to enable Him to realize the creative goal of the human race. This argument is very much like the first. Much must depend on the sense given in this passage to the title *Son of man.* If this is a *Messianic* title, then it implies that the Messiah was already, at the creation, appointed as head of all things, as Westcott holds. But this interpretation involves a misunderstanding both of Psalm 8 and of its quotation in Heb. 2.

In the Psalm we have simply poetic parallelism, *son of man* being equivalent to *man.* Nor does the author of Hebrews change this usage; he repeats the expression as meaning *the human race.* But then he goes on to reflect that we do not yet witness this state of affairs in which all things are made subject to man. Therefore this state is first realized in Christ, but not without sin and redemption. Christ realized it through suffering and death. The creation goal must now be realized by man in a roundabout way, through redemption. Of course it is possible to say that in the beginning God foreknew that it would be realized in this way; but if we are to speak of the foreknowledge of God in this connection, then it must be realized that God's foreknowledge included also the *sin* which followed.

Again, even if all these considerations were to be discounted, still it must be remembered that there is in this passage no mention of the office of priesthood, but only of the kingship or royal rule of Christ.

In 5:1 we are given a statement of what a priest *does*: he acts for man in things pertaining to God, and he brings both gifts and sacrifices for sins (*doora te kai thusias huper hamartioon*). Some variant readings omit the *te* in this verse; if the *te* be omitted, then the word *sins* (*hamartioon*) must be regarded as going with both the nouns, *gifts* (*doora*) and *sacrifices* (*thusias*). But if the *te* belongs in the text, which is the more probable reading, then we have here two separate parts of the function of a priest, namely, the bringing of gifts, and the offering of sacrifices for sin. In that case, the bringing of gifts is independent of sin. It is to this exegesis that Westcott appeals. He regards this, indeed, as the strongest passage in support of his view, since this passage mentions the office of priesthood by name.

Still, to follow Westcott's interpretation involves a misunderstanding of the author of the Epistle. We have no right to infer that the gifts mentioned have nothing to do with sin; we may properly infer only that they have nothing to do with the *removal* of sin. Yet even in connection with these gifts, the priesthood is quite necessary because of the fact of sin, since the fact of sin has resulted in God being inaccessible to man as such. Man in himself is unclean; therefore he needs a priest to bring these gifts in his stead. The passage therefore falls short of proving that there would be a priesthood even apart from sin and redemption.

Finally, over against this, there is the very convincing argument that the author of Hebrews always emphasizes the sinlessness of Christ as a necessary qualification for His priesthood. This is brought out in 4:15, "in all points tempted like as we are, *yet without sin.*" The phrase *without sin* is included to safeguard Christ's perfection. In 7:26 we read: "For such a high priest became us, holy, guileless, undefiled, separated from sinners, and made higher than the heavens." Here again the fact of Christ's sinlessness is brought directly into connection with His priesthood. Again in 7:27, 28 Christ's sinlessness is stressed in connection with His priesthood. In these verses, strangely enough, the very *possession* of sin is mentioned as a necessary qualification of the Old Testament priesthood; but that which in the Old Testament type served as a help to the priestly office, in the New Testament antitype would be a hindrance. Because of his sin the Old Testament high priest could be a better priest — he could *metriopathein* (5:2; on the meaning of this word, see below); but in 7:27 Christ is represented as better qualified, because He does not need to offer daily sacrifices, first for His own sins and then for the sins of the people.

The term *metriopathein* has been variously interpreted. Calvin and the Authorized Version confuse it with *sumpathein.* Calvin translates, "Who can have compassion with the ignorant and erring." Beza and the Dutch version have a better rendering: *Die behoorlijk medelijden kan hebben* — "no lack of sympathetic emotion" — that is to say, Christ is not like a Stoic, who is *apathein* (*devoid of emotion*). The expression used in 5:2, however, is even stronger than this, and is accurately translated in the Revised Version: "who can bear gently with the ignorant and erring" — that is, *who has no excess of indignation.* The term *metriopathein* cannot be used of Christ; He can only be said to *sumpathein,* since He is Himself without sin.

The Epistle presents a complex of four ideas suggested by the *sympathy* of the high priest. These are: (1) suffering; (2) temptation; (3) sympathy; and (4) being perfected.

The passages in which these are brought out are: 2:10, 17, 18; 4:15, 16; 5:7-10; 7:28.

In 2:10 the general thought is that it was fitting that God should make Christ perfect through suffering. Some take the idea in this verse as being equivalent to that in verse 9, "because of the suffering of death crowned with glory and honor." But there is a difference between this statement and that of verse 10, for in verse 9 we find the preposition *dia* with the accusative case, whereas in verse 10 it is used with the genitive case. Moreover in verse 9 the noun *suffering* is in the singular, whereas in verse 10 it is used in the plural. In verse 9 the idea is expressed that the crowning with glory is a *reward* for the suffering. But in verse 10 the suffering is regarded as a school through which Christ went as a process of attaining perfection. How this suffering made Him perfect is not further set forth here. According to some interpreters Christ stood in need of *moral* improvement, but we may regard this as excluded in the nature of the case. The commonest interpretation is that through suffering Christ was made better fitted for His work. This interpretation, however, is subdivided into two views. First, it is said by some to have reference to our Lord's *emotional* life, so that His experience of pain led to His relieving *our* pain. Second, it is taken by others as relating more to the moral life of our Lord; the meaning then is that Christ comes to see how suffering itself involves temptation and so brings a moral danger; Christ's sympathy therefore extends to a relief of our *moral* weakness, because of the temptation which was suggested to Him in His suffering. As to which of these interpretations is the correct one, this passage taken by itself does not afford data for an answer.

Turning to 2:17,18, we read: "Wherefore it behooved him in all things to be made like unto his brethren, that he might become a merciful and faithful high priest in things pertaining to God. . . ." Here the idea of sympathy is suggested, and also that of suffering, in Christ's being made like unto His brethren. The next clause makes it plain that the purpose in view was that of making expiation for the sins of the people. The mercy here extended is to the moral weakness of His brethren. This mercy is therefore a continuous state of mind exercised now by Christ in heaven. The reference is not to the sacrifice of Calvary, but to the intercessory work of Christ as priest which is now being exercised in heaven. In verse 18 this is further brought out by the statement that "he is able to succor them that are tempted." Note the somewhat complicated construction in verse 18. The Authorized and Revised Versions in the text read: "for in that he himself hath suffered being tempted . . ." This would suggest that the suffering proceeded from the fact of being tempted, that is, that temptation is itself a form of suffering. But the marginal rendering of the Revised Version is much better: "For having been himself tempted in that wherein he hath suffered." This translation represents the temptation as proceeding *from the suffering* rather than *vice versa*.

In 4:15,16 we have the same thought, namely that of a high priest who is touched with the feeling of our infirmities. Note especially the force of *gar* at the beginning of verse 15. The contemplation of Christ's greatness in verse 14 might lead people to have lofty ideas of Him as One who could not have any feeling for them; therefore the author goes on to assure them: "For (*gar*) we have not a high priest that cannot be touched with the feeling of our infirmities. . . ."

The term *infirmities* might seem ambiguous here. It might mean *sinful infirmities*. It would be a rather euphemistic expression for this, however, though we do find examples of such usage in Scripture, as e.g., in Psalm 77:10. But this is not the meaning in Heb. 4:15, where it designates rather *natural weaknesses*. To be sure, these natural weaknesses rendered Christ subject to temptations, yet they were not sinful in themselves. It is on this basis that the author could so emphasize Christ's likeness to us, which he could not have done if the reference had been to our sinful infirmities. Like Christ, we are tempted by the natural weaknesses of humanity; the difference between Him and us is only in the outcome of the temptations. We have all sinned; He remained without sin. There was just as much real *appeal* to sin for Him as there is with us, but in His case there was no *issue* of sin. Thus we can see the meaning of the statement about Christ being touched with the feeling of our infirmities. This is further borne out by verse 16; we need, not only *mercy*, in the general sense of pity or compassion, but also specifically *grace*, as a moral factor, as mercy extended to sinners.

Turning now to 5:7-10, we observe that this passage does not deal with the question we are considering directly. Still by implication it involves it with great richness. The high priest must be called of God. To show that this is true also of Christ, the author dwells on His *preparation*. He shows that Christ did not usurp His office, but became perfect (*teleios*) through a process of preparation for it. One of the aims of this preparation was for Him to become identified with His people in the matter of *learning obedience*. This goes beyond the previous passage, therefore, in mentioning not merely the negative factor of resisting temptation, but also the positive factor of *obedience*. Christ learned obedience in order to become the author of eternal salvation to all that obey Him. Thus He is prepared for His office not only by acquaintance with weakness, but also by the exercise of strength.

Note the play on the Greek words in the original text of 5:8: *emathen aph' hoon epathen ten hupakoen*. Incidentally, this phenomenon confirms the view that the Epistle was originally written in Greek, for such a play on words would be very unlikely to occur in a document translated from another language into Greek.

Note that the obedience referred to was in the way of suffering, that is, it was an obedience which conquered the *disinclination* to suffering. This period of Christ's preparation is called *the days of his flesh*. He had to conquer, then, *the fear of death*, offering up prayers and supplications to be saved from (i.e., out of) death, that He might not be held of death.

Here *learning* is not equivalent to acquiring something new, as if He would only have the obedience after learning it. For in that case He would have been imperfect before the learning took place. Compare 10:7, "Then said I, Lo, I am come. . . to do thy will, O God." This implies that from the beginning there was the principle of obedience in Him. Therefore in 5:8 *learning obedience* signifies *bringing out into the present conscious experience of action* that which was already present in principle. There is a great difference, of course, between the mere principle and even the desire to obey, and the actual carrying out of the desire.

Note also the article with the noun *obedience* in the Greek of 5:8: *ten hupakoen*. This is a generic article. The meaning is that Christ learned what obedience meant in its inner essence. Note further that it is said that *though he was a Son, yet he learned obedience*. The contrast is not between *Son* and *obedience,* as though it were strange for a son to be obedient, but rather between *Sonship* and having to learn obedience *through suffering,* which was unnatural for one who was a Son.

As to the term *perfection* (*teleioosis*), we must adhere strictly to the meaning *fitting for the office*. The experience of learning was a moral experience, to be sure; but the perfection attained was not moral perfection, but a perfect fitness for His office.

In 7:28 we read: "For the law appointeth men high priests, having infirmity; but the word of the oath, which was after the law, appointeth a Son, perfected for evermore." The reference here is to the sinful infirmities of the Old Testament priests. But note further: "but the word of the oath, which was after the law, appointeth a Son, perfected for evermore." This would tend to suggest the paraphrase: "a Son *made perfect and so* without infirmity." Yet in verses 26, 27 the affirmation of Christ's sinless perfection renders this idea impossible. The solution lies in the right paraphrasing. The meaning is: the men appointed by the law had sin and infirmity; but the word of the oath appointed a Son, who not only has no sin, but even has been made *perfect,* namely, in obedience (as was brought out in 5:7-10).

So much for the *humanity* of Christ as a qualification for His priesthood.

Christ's *deity* also has a bearing on His priesthood, however. We have already dwelt on the importance of the Sonship as brought out in 1:3. Note that in that passage the priestly office also stands under the ontological Sonship; it stands in an intermediate position between the offices of prophet and king: ". . . upholding all things by the word of his power, *when he had made purification of sins,* sat down on the right hand of the Majesty on high." In 3:6 we read of Christ being set over the whole house of God, as a Son. Because He was a Son, He was also set over the priestly functions of the house of God. In 4:14 He is called *a great high priest* because He is *Jesus the Son of God.* In 5:5 we read, "Christ also glorified not himself to be made a high priest, but he that spake unto him, Thou art my Son, this day have I begotten thee." No one may usurp the office of high priest, which includes a great honor. Even Christ did not take this honor Himself; it was given to Him by God, who said to Him, *Thou art my Son.* Thus the priestly honor is the outcome of the higher honor of the divine Sonship. In 7:28 the Sonship contributes to the perfection of the priesthood. Note the twofold contrast here: (1) one who is *a Son* is contrasted with *men;* (2) one who learned obedience and *was perfected* is contrasted with those who *had infirmity.* The first of these contrasts refers to Christ's ontological Sonship.

Within the sphere of Christ's deity, the author of Hebrews further singles out His *eternity* as a special attribute. This is especially brought out in chapter 7, in the comparison of Christ with Melchizedek. Melchizedek was made like unto Christ in the latter's eternity, 7:3. The Son of God, therefore, by His own nature, determines His own priesthood. But how does He effect this? In the first place, the general greatness of Christ must be reckoned with, as shown by 7:4,7. Christ is a great figure, even greater than Melchizedek. More particularly, however, the one attribute dwelt upon is that of His *eternity*. But how could Melchizedek be called an *eternal* figure? Some think that this is to be taken in the literal sense, as signifying an eternity in both directions, past as well as future. This interpretation must of necessity regard Melchizedek not merely as a supernatural being, but even as a *divine being*. Then Melchizedek must be the Son of God Himself. There is nothing inherently impossible in such a view. But the context excludes it, for Melchizedek is said to be "made *like unto* the Son of God," which must exclude the idea of his actually *being* the Son of God. In the original reference to Melchizedek in Gen. 14:18 ff. he is also compared with Abraham, as also himself a man. Thus we cannot *a priori* affirm that Melchizedek is a divine being, because eternity is ascribed to him in the Epistle to the Hebrews.

If Melchizedek's eternity is attached to his priesthood, it would mean that there is no end to his priesthood. But in that case his priesthood would encroach on that of Christ, both in function and in place, being necessarily exercised also in heaven, if it is literally eternal. But such an interpretation would certainly be contrary to the teaching of the Epistle. Therefore only one possible interpretation remains, namely the view that while Melchizedek was an historical person and not eternal, still as a Scriptural figure he was regarded as eternal, being without recorded father or mother or genealogy, and having no recorded beginning of days nor end of life. In these respects he is like unto the Son of God, that is, stripped of all earthly attachments. As such, then, he is also a type of Christ. Thus *as he appears in Scriptures* he may be regarded as enveloped in an atmosphere of eternity.

This implies that what is further said of him is not to be applied to him in the matter of the priesthood exclusively. While the mention of his being without father might refer simply to his priesthood, the statement that he was also *without mother* and the statement about his "having neither beginning of days nor end of life," clearly cannot refer exclusively to his priesthood. To try to limit the reference in this way would amount to drawing the comparison back from the figurative into the realistic sphere. What is affirmed of Melchizedek in Heb. 7, then, is affirmed of him *in his typical appearance.*

In this purely typical sense his eternity could well be affirmed in both directions, past as well as future. This would be equally true of Melchizedek as the type and of Christ Himself. But if we limit the reference to the priesthood, then what is said of Melchizedek cannot even be affirmed of Christ, namely that he was eternal in both directions, since Christ's priestly office had its beginning on earth in time. The idea therefore is that the priestly dignity is derived from the personal dignity. In Christ's case the personal factor was the decisive factor.

How then does this eternity shape the priesthood? With respect to the eternity we are not first of all to think of the factor of *duration.* The Greek word *aioonios* has a double meaning. Here it has especially the connotation of *power,* of having the energy or the dynamic of the eternal world. This may be observed in 7:15 ff. In verses 15-19 the author first dwells on the fact of Christ's power; then, as a second thought, from verse 19 on, he speaks of the eternal duration of Christ's power and priesthood. Note verse 16, *after the power of an endless life* (Revised Version margin, *an indissoluble life*). This line of connection is not so clearly drawn by Paul in his epistles. While Paul speaks of the resurrected Christ, he does not dwell on the inherent active power which made His resurrection necessary. Paul emphasizes rather the passive side of the resurrection, speaking of Christ more as *raised* from the dead. Here in Hebrews the active idea enters, and it is stated that death could not dissolve the life in Christ, because of His attribute of eternity which gave Him such power.

In verses 23-25 the second effect of Christ's eternity, namely His endless duration, is shown in the sphere of life. The Old Testament priests were many in number, because death continually took them away, but Christ abides forever. Therefore Christ is able to save *to the uttermost* — to the uttermost, not in degree, but in point of *time* — those that draw near unto God through Him.

The next question is, at what point does the author regard Christ's priesthood as beginning, that is, at what point of time and in what locality? On the one hand it is claimed that the work of Christ on earth must have formed part of His priestly ministry, and on the other hand it has been observed that His priesthood is especially associated with His entry into heaven. This dispute assumed dogmatic importance in a controversy about the doctrine of the atonement. The Socinians opposed the vicarious doctrine of the atonement, therefore they tried to detach the death of Christ from His priestly functions. Consequently they regarded Christ's priesthood as beginning *after* His death, and they also would not allow Christ's death to color the meaning of His priesthood. They kept the two conceptions — Christ's death and His priesthood — quite distinct. Christ's priesthood, then, according to the Socinians, became simply a general position of influence with God. But today we are no longer under this dogmatic necessity of determining the point where Christ's priesthood begins. More thorough exegesis since the days of the Socinian controversy has shown that no matter where Christ's priesthood begins, it can, in any case, not be detached from His death. This is agreed upon by practically all scholars. Christ's death and His activity in heaven are organically connected. So far as this problem is concerned, it is a matter of indifference whether we speak of three offices of Christ, namely prophet, priest and king, or whether we add a fourth, that of sacrifice, as following the office of prophet.

Still, the question as to where Christ's priesthood begins remains an interesting one: is Christ's sacrifice a mere passive sacrifice, or is He also the priest who makes the sacrifice? Certain passages seem to favor the view that Christ's priesthood began with His ascension into heaven after His death and resurrection. The first of these passages is 2:17, "made like unto his brethren, that he might become a merciful and faithful high priest. . . " In this verse Christ's high priesthood seems to be placed *after* the experience of earthly life.   We might avoid this interpretation by placing all the emphasis on the words *merciful and faithful*.   Still this is invidious.   The meaning is rather that Christ's earthly life was a school of training for the later priesthood.

In 5:9, 10 we find a similar meaning.   Christ is affirmed to have been made high priest after He became perfect.   This being made perfect consisted in learning obedience by the things which He suffered; after this followed His priesthood.

In 6:20 we find the same idea again.   Christ's entering within the veil marks the moment when He became high priest.   We could again evade the meaning given here by emphasizing the word *forever,* implying that He also was high priest before that, but that at this point He became *eternal* high priest.   But again this is probably not the true meaning.

In 7:26-28 Christ is described as high priest, and the adjectives added seem to apply to Christ's heavenly station, especially the phrase *made higher than the heavens.*   The same thought is also suggested by the clause "the word of the oath . . . appointeth a Son, perfected for evermore."   This represents the perfection and training as lying behind Him.   So also in verses 20, 21, *Thou art a priest for ever,* which is represented as spoken to Christ when He is exalted.

In 8:2 Christ is called "a minister of the sanctuary, and of the true tabernacle, which the Lord pitched, not man" — that is, the tabernacle *in heaven.*   This verse would appear to lead to the same inference, namely that Christ's priesthood began at His ascension.

In 8:4 we find the strongest statement of all: "Now if he were on earth, he would not be a priest at all . . ."

The arguments for the contrary position, that Christ's priesthood existed before His exaltation, during His earthly ministry, are based on the following considerations:

First, the statement of 1:3, which reads: ". . . when he had made purification of sins, sat down on the right hand of the Majesty on high."   It is held that *making purification of sins* was a priestly act, and therefore 1:3 represents Christ's priestly functions as exercised on earth. This, however, is not at all conclusive. The difficulty is that it is impossible to determine with exactness what is meant by this act of purification. It may refer to the atonement on the cross, or it may refer to something else. Elsewhere in the Epistle this act is frequently located in heaven. Therefore it must probably be so interpreted here also, as the offering presented before the Father's throne in heaven.

In 9:11,24 Christ is represented as entering into heaven as high priest. On the basis of this it seems natural to argue that He must have been such *before* entering heaven. But it is also possible that it was precisely the entrance into heaven that made Him high priest.

7:11 asks, "what further need was there that another priest should arise?" The verb here is more naturally understood of a *historical* appearance. If so understood, it must refer to the days of our Lord's earthly ministry. Thus this is the first passage which is at all conclusive for proving that Christ was a priest during His ministry on earth.

In 13:12 we read: "Wherefore Jesus also, that he might sanctify the people through his own blood, suffered without the gate." Unless we interpret this sanctifying as prospective in nature, it must be understood as a priestly act on the part of Christ before His death.

In 10:20 the dissolution of the flesh of Jesus is represented as the dedication of a new and living way. This dedicating is a priestly act, which was performed on the cross.

Passages using the term *offering* (*prospherein*) would be convincing if they could be properly limited to Calvary, but they are not so restricted in this Epistle. Sometimes the offering is referred to heaven. Therefore the context must decide in each case. Thus, for example, in 8:3 the statement about Christ *having somewhat to offer* does not imply an offering on earth, since the next verse clearly speaks of the offering being made in heaven. On the other hand, the word is not confined to the act in heaven. In the LXX *prospherein* is used to translate the Hebrew *hikrith* (from *karath*), and this is used in a very comprehensive way, covering everything from the bringing of the animal to the altar to the actual slaying. In Heb. 9:26-28, however, the term *prospherein* must be applied strictly to the death of Christ: "so Christ also, having been once offered to bear the sins of many, shall appear a second time, apart from sin, to them that wait for him, unto salvation." Here Calvary and heaven are linked. This is brought out, first, by the passive participle, *having been offered*. In heaven Christ's offering is not passive but active. Still, how does this prove that He was more than a mere sacrifice here on earth? That He was more than a mere sacrifice on earth is shown by the context, verse 26: "now once at the end of the ages hath he been manifested to put away sin by the sacrifice of himself." This necessarily refers to the earthly, historic sphere. Therefore Christ must have acted as a priest on Calvary, before His death. A two-fold appearance is involved, including one appearance before His death, as is also brought out by the comparison in verse 27: "it is appointed unto men once to die, and after this cometh judgment."

The actual exercise of the priesthood of Christ probably cannot be traced farther back than His death. As for the word *prospherein,* this is used not only of a sacrifice of animals, but also of an offering up of prayer, so that the word has become quite general in its meaning.

The question now before us is, how are the two representations of Christ's priesthood related to each other? It is held by some that the author of Hebrews sets forth *two orders* of priesthood, namely the order of Aaron and the order of Melchizedek. The order of Aaron would then be the earthly priesthood, and that of Melchizedek would be the heavenly priesthood. This view is set forth by Bruce in his Humiliation of Christ, though he does not repeat it in his commentary on Hebrews. It is also Riehm's view. There is nothing in the Epistle, however, that really lends support to such a view. It is difficult to show how the Old Testament priesthood, before Christ's death, fell short of the ministry of Melchizedek.

It might be argued that the Aaronic priesthood lacked the true eternity. Still, the author does not look upon the sacrifice of death as terminating the priesthood, but rather just as marking its exercise. And if the word *eternity* is taken to mean an eternity of *power,* then Christ's priesthood is also fully equal to that of Melchizedek. It is also impossible to cut loose the ministry and sacrifice on earth from the presenting of the offering in heaven. We cannot say that the *bringing* of the offering was characteristic of Aaron, while the *presenting* of it was characteristic of Melchizedek. Bruce also felt the force of this consideration, and therefore he adopted the strange view that the Aaronic order of priesthood continues until the presenting of the sacrifice in heaven, at which point only the order of Melchizedek begins. But in that case we face the difficulty as to what substance is left to the order of Melchizedek. It then becomes merely a priesthood of prayer in our behalf. If we make the distinction purely one of time and space, then we are not fully adjusted to the author's point of view, for he did not think in terms of our ordinary chronology and geography.

Our difficulty lies further in not having defined with sufficient accuracy what is meant by priesthood. It may mean either *appointment* or *function*. If it means the latter, then the former would surely have to precede it. The question then is, where did each of these begin? In the sense of *function* it is quite possible to assert that Christ is priest only in heaven. But in His *appointment* He was a priest while still on earth. This involves no real contradiction, since the term *priesthood* is used with two different meanings.

Still further, it has not been sufficiently defined which part of the priestly function is exercised in heaven. What is the core or essence of this function? We have found that this consists in His bringing near to God by establishing contact with God through His death. Now if reference is had to everything necessary to this, then much must be included which is not essential to the culminating act which is the main thing, namely the establishing of the contact. But if the work is limited to *the purpose of the act,* then the priest-hood is confined to heaven. For in this realization of the pur-pose lies the climax. Then the two forms of statement can be held without contradiction.

The second defect lies in the fact that the question is too mechanically formulated as to time and place. For this too mechanical formulation there should be substituted the con-cept of *the sanctuary,* and it should be asked where this was and when it was established. This brings the act out of the sphere of abstractions into the realm of the concrete. And this is certainly what the author had in mind. We must inquire, not *Where did Christ die?,* but rather, *Where was the sanc-tuary which was held in view in His death?* Thus we get a ritual reference to His death. This statement involves, not ordinary geographical conceptions, but those of a *ritual ge-ography.* It embodies an ideal reference to the heavenly sanc-tuary. This may appear most clearly from 8:4: "Now if he were on earth, he would not be a priest at all, seeing there are those who offer the gifts according to the law." If we take this as a bald geographical statement, then the priesthood of Christ is entirely removed from the earth. But the meaning is rather that if Christ had the *center* of His priesthood, that is, His *sanctuary,* on earth, He would not be a priest at all. The author in this verse by no means states or implies that Christ could not *act* as a priest on earth, but only that He could not really *be* a priest on earth.

This is made still clearer by the analogy from the Old Tes-tament. The author compares the ministry of Christ with the ministry of the Old Testament high priest, and particularly with the latter's act on the annual Day of Atonement. Christ's ministry is represented as the counterpart of this ritual. Un-der the old covenant, the high priest had his business only with the Holy of Holies; that was specifically the locality of his activities. Still, on the Day of Atonement he had to per-form also the act of slaying the sacrificial animal in the court before the sanctuary. This slaying was therefore not a menial act, or it would have been performed by an ordinary priest instead of by the high priest. It was a distinctly priestly act. This corresponds exactly with Christ's priestly act, which He performed outside the sanctuary, that is, outside of heaven, on Calvary. This one act does not lower the priesthood nor does it in any way imply that the true location of that priesthood is the heavenly sanctuary. Again, as the Old Testament act was performed with reference to the Holy of Holies, so Christ's act on Calvary had its ideal reference to the sanctuary in heaven.

Still further, it is to be remembered that according to the author, heaven and earth more or less intermingle for the Christian. The Christian already anticipates his heavenly state here on earth. But if this is true of believers, as a merely redemptive acquisition, how much more must it be true of Christ, who is Himself directly *a heavenly Person?* The act, therefore, was performed in the *milieu* of heaven, since Christ Himself was a piece of heaven come down to earth. Note the statement in 9:14, ". . . Christ, who through the eternal Spirit offered himself without blemish unto God. . . ." This does not refer to the Holy Spirit, but to the Spirit which was His own, that is, to *Christ's divine nature.* Also, the word *eternal* here means *heavenly.* Therefore the meaning is that *through the heavenly aspect of His deity* Christ makes the offering. This is also borne out by the opening words of the Epistle: ". . . the Son, after he had made propitiation of sins in himself." The verb here is in the middle voice, which is significant, indicating something taking place *within Christ's Person.*

*The Better Sacrifice:*
*The Sacrifice of the New Covenant*

# CHAPTER V

## THE BETTER SACRIFICE: THE SACRIFICE OF THE NEW COVENANT

The sacrifice is the center of Christ's priestly work. Yet there is no formulated doctrine of the atonement, such as we might expect to find, presented in this Epistle. Much more of that character is found in the Epistles of Paul, though Paul never speaks of Christ as a priest or sacrifice. Why is there so much stress on priesthood and sacrifice in Hebrews, while the atonement is not mentioned? The author speaks in Old Testament terms, using the symbolic language of the Old Testament, which contains the doctrine within it in picture form. Therefore the author of Hebrews also speaks of Christ as priest and sacrifice, and says but little about the theory or doctrine behind these symbolic representations.

Secondly, the aim of the Epistle also includes the fact that the author is more interested in the result of the sacrifice than its mode and progress. Therefore the *method* of the sacrifice recedes into the background. But the *doctrine* of the atonement has to do with the method, and therefore it is not found here.

Some writers have drawn from this fact the conclusion that the author had no doctrine of the atonement. This is a great mistake, however. The author has been branded a ritualist because he speaks of cleansing, sanctifying, and the like. Thus it is alleged that the author felt no further need of the inner significance of the ritual, but thought of the external act as sanctifying him, without inquiring into the explanation of the act. The objection to this, however, is that everywhere else in the Epistle we find precisely the opposite of the above, namely, extreme spiritualizing in speaking of the act of

Christ, as compared with the Old Testament sacrifices. The whole tenor of the Epistle, therefore, is directly away from ritualism.

A third view is that the author had a doctrine of the atonement, but a different one from that of Paul, due to a difference in his conception of sin. Because of this difference in the conception of sin, his conception of the corrective of sin would be different too. For Paul sin is said to be transgression, demanding a vicarious satisfaction as a corrective. But the Epistle to the Hebrews is alleged to have a different conception, speaking of sin rather as defilement, the effect of which is not so much God's displeasure, as exclusion from His sanctuary. Therefore, it is said, the applicable corrective is not a vicarious satisfaction, but rather cleansing, sanctifying, rendering fit for worship.

The objection to this view is as follows: in the first place, it is not logical to contrast these two conceptions in this way, setting them over against each other and calling them both *doctrines* of the atonement, or *theories* of the atonement. Paul's language does indeed admit of being called a *doctrine* or *theory,* giving us literal expressions. But the language of Hebrews is metaphorical, and therefore cannot be called a doctrine or theory. To say *that blood cleanses* is clearly a metaphor. Before we can affirm that Paul and Hebrews present two doctrines or theories of the atonement, then, this metaphorical language must first be translated into other terms. But when this has been done, it will be seen that the result is not another, divergent theory or doctrine of the atonement, but one identical with that of Paul.

It is further sometimes stated that Paul finds in the death of Christ an *objective* effect, while in Hebrews the atonement is represented as having a *subjective* effect, namely, the cleansing of man. This again is due to a total misunderstanding of the Epistle. For when the author says that we are cleansed, etc., in no case is he thinking of something which takes place within the personality of the believer. Rather, the author means the very same thing that Paul means by the term *jus-*

*tification,* and the conception of cleansing in Hebrews is just as objective as is that of justification in Paul. For what is cleansed? But what is taken away when our conscience is cleansed? Not the *stain* of sin, but the *guilt* of sin.

Now taking up the positive side of the argument that the author has a doctrine of the atonement in the background of his mind, this follows from the fact that the author finds a *reasonableness* in Christ's sufferings, which implies his having a doctrine. True, he sometimes seems to attribute Christ's death purely to the will of God (the Scotist view), which would represent the death as having no *inherent* value. Note the statements of 10:5,9,10. The Messiah received a body in order that He might be able to die. He received it that by dying He might fulfil the will of God. And in this will we are sanctified. Still, the author does not mean to represent this will as an arbitrary will. But God preferred this to the blood of bulls and goats. Preference involves reasonableness, and reasonableness involves a theory behind it. There is also an *a posteriori* argument: *How much more* will He not save us? This *how much more* again implies a reason behind it. Therefore there was reason in the process from the beginning.

The same statement is found in 2:10, *For it became him* . . . Decorum is therefore involved, and the reason for this is also added, namely that it was necessary for realizing God's world-plan. The warrant for Christ's sacrifice was the will of God. And in Him we have the warrant that nothing shall be done that is not fitting. A further warrant for this still lies in His leading many sons to glory. There are two elements, therefore, that contribute to our understanding of the reasonableness of the act.

These passages, however, still do not define the rationale of the sacrificial act of Christ. This is brought out in the passages which we shall now proceed to consider.

The first of these passages is 9:12. Christ through His blood obtained eternal redemption (*lutroosis*). Here we have not a mere figure, as in the cases where we read of blood cleansing, etc. Here there is given the answer to the question as to *how* the blood can give entrance into heaven: it is *through redemption.* This is a forensic Pauline term. Verse 15 gives the same word: redemption from the sins of the first *Diatheke.* Of course it was not *the sins* that were redeemed. The genitive here is a genitive of separation, meaning *redemption away from sin,* sin being here personified. Here again we are on Pauline ground. The sin holds us in *bondage,* requiring atonement by the sacrifice of Christ. Verse 28 is still more explicit, again using Pauline language: Christ is offered up for the bearing (*enengkein*) of the sins of many. Here the ritual and the forensic formula meet together. It is here not merely vaguely stated that Christ *removes* the sin: it is plainly stated that *He takes it upon Himself.* Note the expression *shall apear a second time, apart from sin.* . . (9:28). The verb *enengkein* is literally taken from the LXX of Isa. 53, which is a purely vicarious passage. Compare 1 Pet. 2:24, "who his own self bare our sins in his body upon the tree" (*anenengkein*).

The next passage which we must consider is 2:14,15. Christ through death brought to nought him that had the power of death. Note the emphasis in the original on the word *death,* which stands first in the sentence. Death, therefore, is abolished through death, which is clearly a vicarious act. Other explanations, however, have been offered for this passage. The fathers held the theory that the ransom was paid *to Satan.* Another explanation suggested by some of them was that Satan had exceeded his rights; he had been permitted by God the Father to torment the people, but not Christ. These are fanciful conceptions, of course. Still the question remains, why is Satan mentioned here at all? The answer is furnished by the context. The passage moves in the world of Paradise. The eighth Psalm is quoted in this connection. And it is in this connection that the writer comes to speak of the devil, since the devil was so prominent in the beginning of the world's history. The fear of death, however, is now not a retrospective fear; rather, it lies in the torments of the future life, in which the devil still has his hand. And from this Christ by His death now delivers us.

## The Ritual Terminology

There are four terms employed in the Epistle to express the effect of Christ's sacrifice. These are *hilaskesthai* (*to expiate*); *katharizein* (*to purify*); *hagiazein* (*to sanctify*); *teleioun* (*to perfect*).

*Hilaskesthai* occurs only once, in 2:17: ". . . that he might become a merciful and faithful high priest in things pertaining to God, *to make propitiation* for the sins of the people." This word was used by pagan classical writers also. For them, however, it always has *the gods* as its object. In Hebrews, however, it has *the sins* as its object. In the classical pagan usage, the meaning was to placate or pacify the gods. Clearly this idea gives no sense with reference to sin; we cannot speak of placating or pacifying sin. The author, therefore, uses the word not in its original sense, but in the sense which it has in the usage of the LXX. There it serves to translate the Hebrew *kipper*, which means *to cover*. The usage in Hebrews differs slightly from that of the Old Testament, however, for in the Old Testament it was *the persons* that were covered, whereas in Hebrews it is *the sins* that are covered. There is one text in the Old Testament, however, which corresponds exactly with the idea in Heb. 2:17, namely Psalm 65:3 (verse 4 in the Hebrew): "As for our transgressions, thou wilt *expiate* them" (Revised Version margin).

*Katharizein* occurs several times; the noun form of this word is found in 1:3, and the verb form in 9:14,22,23; 10:2. This is the term that is most easily misleading, leading us to think of an ethical operation. But such is not the meaning; rather, it signifies *to clear of guilt, to purify the guilt away.* This act can sometimes be purely declarative. The priest, for instance, was to purify a person of his leprosy, which was a purely external declaration, of course, not an internal act performed by the priest.

Note further that it is not the Spirit that is represented as purifying, but *the blood*. Therefore the meaning clearly is that of *purifying of guilt*. Thus it is equivalent to *kipper* (*to cover*). Compare Job 7:21, "And why dost thou not pardon my transgression, and take away mine iniquity?" The priest, therefore, makes purification of sins, which of course does not mean making the sins clean, but rather signifies *a purifying removal of sin*. Compare with this the form of statement found in the Gospels, *his leprosy was cleansed* (*purified*), that is, purged away.

Notice also the plural in Heb. 1:3: purification of *sins*. If it were an ethical operation, sin would be expressed as a unity, and the singular would be used, not the plural. But in the forensic purifications the single items of guilt must be considered. Note still further that the form of the verb is the aorist participle, implying an act performed once for all and not repeated. And finally note that it is in the middle voice: "having made *in himself* purification of sins . . ." The *di' heautou* in the text is very likely a later gloss, though one which sets forth the true meaning; yet it is really superfluous, because the middle voice of the verb, which is employed, itself conveys the same idea as is conveyed by the phrase *di' heautou*.

In 9:14 the *purpose* of the act is also added, namely, *to serve the living God*. The meaning is that Christ takes away the hindrances to this service. The reference is therefore not to the ethical state of mind of the worshippers, but rather to the forensic side, namely to the removal of disqualifications for worship.

In 10:2 it is a matter of having or not having a consciousness of sin. This plainly refers to the guilt of the sin. In 9:22,23 the objects that are purified are named — they are the utensils of worship, the altar, and so forth. Therefore here again it is not an ethical transformation that is referred to.

We shall now consider the verb *hagiazein*. We may easily be misled as to the meaning of this word, because of the distinction elsewhere between this word (*sanctify*) and *justification*. This distinction does not hold here, however. There is only one passage in Hebrews in which the Pauline idea of *sanctification* occurs, namely 12:14. The other passages containing the word are 2:11; 9:13; 10:10,14,29; 13:12.

Up to a certain point *sanctifying* is entirely synonymous with *purifying*, only it goes further in meaning. In the case of *purifying* the further modification *to serve the living God* must be added; but in the case of *sanctifying* this modification need not be added, for the idea is already included in the connotation of *sanctify*. The word contains both the negative idea of *purifying from sin* and the positive idea of *serving God*. This also, acccording to 10:10, takes place once for all.

The usage in 2:11 may perhaps seem to be different from this: "For both he that sanctifieth and they that are sanctified are all of one . . ." But in this verse the meaning of *they that are sanctified* is not that they are *being sanctified* by a continuous process; rather, the author intends to present a characteristic description of them, comparing those affected by this sanctifying with Him who effects it.

Coming now to the word *teleioun*, the meaning of this word in the Christological passages previously cited should be compared. In those passages there is never any reference to *moral perfection*, but always to a *fitting for office*. With reference to believers, the word is *soteriologically* considered. The passages are: 7:11, 19; 9:9; 10:1, 14; 11:40; 12:23. The first four passages listed are negative, stating that the Old Testament could not render perfect, and therefore implying that the new *Diatheke* does render perfect, meaning that it prepares for the goal. This goal is always the service of God. In this respect therefore *teleioun* is equivalent to *hagiazein*, adding the note of a positive purpose. This is seen from the object given to the verb. In nearly all passages it is *the worshippers*, those that draw nigh. It represents therefore the opposite to the Old Testament disability; it is the bringing in of a better hope, namely, to draw near to God. In 10:1,2 the purpose of *teleioun* is implied, namely, that the worshippers should have no further consciousness of sin.

The next passage to be considered is 11:39,40. Here the perfecting effected by Christ is carried back to the Old Testament believers. Thus a retroactive effect is ascribed to the work of Christ. These Old Testament believers were not affected, however, until Christ actually entered upon His sacrifice. They waited through the ages for this. They did not receive the promise in their own lifetime, this being reserved for us, that they should not be made perfect without us. This implies, of course, that *now* they too have been made perfect.

There is a dispute about the clause *God having provided some better thing concerning us.* The question at issue is, *better than what?* The first view is: better by comparison with what the Old Testament believers received in their time, which was *a prospect* of perfecting. According to this view, the better thing provided for us is *not having to wait* for perfecting. A second view is: what the New Testament believers actually received is better than *what they would have received* if the Old Testament believers had been made perfect at once, without having to wait. Had that been the case, the world would have come to an end, and the readers of the Epistle would never have been born. In this view the better thing was the postponement of the perfection of the Old Testament believers until the New Testament believers could have an opportunity to be born. The first of these two interpretations is obviously the preferable one.

All these terms describe the atonement not from the point of view of its intrinsic essence, but from the point of view of its forensic effect. In Paul it is just the opposite: the effect is treated from the point of view of what happens in the atonement intrinsically. This viewing of the atonement *exclusively in its effect* is an important distinguishing characteristic of the Epistle to the Hebrews.